Becoming an Unstoppable WOMAN Entrepreneur

26 POWERHOUSE
INDUSTRY LEADING WOMEN

© 2022 ALL RIGHTS RESERVED. Published by Heart Centered Women Publishing www.HeartCenteredWomenPublishing.com in collaboration with She Rises Studios www.SheRisesStudios.com and the Co-Authors in this book.

No part of this book may be reproduced or transmitted in any form whatsoever, electronic, or mechanical, including photocopying, recording, or by any informational storage or retrieval system without the expressed written, dated and signed permission from the publisher and co-authors.

LIMITS OF LIABILITY / DISCLAIMER OF WARRANTY:

The co-authors and publisher of this book have used their best efforts in preparing this material. While every attempt has been made to verify information provided in this book, neither the co-authors nor the publisher assumes any responsibility for any errors, omissions or inaccuracies.

The co-authors and publisher make no representation or warranties with respect to the accuracy, applicability, or completeness of the contents of this book. They disclaim any warranties (expressed or implied), merchantability, or for any purpose. The co-authors and publisher shall in no event be held liable for any loss or other damages, including but not limited to special, incidental, consequential, or other damages.

Table of Contents

Introduction 1

Young & Sassy! by Adriana Luna Carlos 6

A Girl With A Dream by Hanna Olivas 13

YOU are your biggest asset! by Michèle Kline 20

Say Yes To being YOU! by Nicole Curtis 27

Changing the Chatter by Alicia Marcos Birong 33

I am Charly by Charly Niesen 41

What Being An Entrepreneur Means To Me by Pamela Kurt 47

Conquering My Journey by Lovely LaGuerre 54

Build Your Brand Like A Boss by Krystal Vernee' 61

Turning Passion into Purpose by Aileen V. Sicat 67

The Conquering Goddess: Balancing the Warrior and the Wizard by Alyson MacLeod 73

A ZunZún Within by Roxana Valeton 79

Lady Rebel Club: Start of a Revolution by Jennifer Cairns 85

Living the Dream by Natalie Pickett 92

Love, Truth and Being a Female Entrepreneur by Valerie Carrillo ... 99

How to Bloom in business and life by Lisa Shepherd 105

Get Out of Your Own Way by Danielle Archer 112

I Quit… Again! by Gayle Gunn 119

Stay in Your Lane! by Laura Croce 125

Your Business Can Be Successful! by Jenny Ngo 131

Faith, Focus and Financial Growth by Heather Stokes 139

Work Like a Woman, Get Paid Like a Man by Lauren Weiss 145

Building Your Resilience by Melissa Porterfield 152

Mom Boss Rising: Live Your Dream Life by Olivia Radcliffe 158

The Keys to Be Me by Priya Ali 165

Self-Made Female Entrepreneur by Charlotte Howard Collins 171

Introduction

She Rises Studios was created and inspired by mother-daughter duo Hanna Olivas and Adriana Luna Carlos. In the middle of 2020 when the world was at one of its most vulnerable times, we saw the need to embrace women globally by offering inspirational quotes, blogs, and articles. Then, in March of 2021, we launched our very own Women's Empowerment Podcast: She Rises Studios Podcast.

It is now one of the most sought out Women's based podcasts both nationally and internationally. You can find us on any of your favorite podcast platforms, such as Spotify, Google Podcasts, Apple Podcasts, IHeartRadio, and much more! We didn't stop there. The need to establish a safe space for women has become an even deeper need. Women lost their businesses, employment, homes, finances, spouses, and more to a global pandemic.

That's when we decided to form the She Rises Studios Community Facebook Group. An environment strictly for women about women. Our focus in this group is to educate and celebrate women globally. To meet them exactly where they are on their journey.

It's a group of Ordinary Women Doing EXTRAordinary Things..

As we continued to grow our network, we saw a need to help shape the minds and influences of women struggling with insecurities, doubts, fears, etc. From this, we created a global movement known as:

Introduction

Becoming An Unstoppable Woman

#BAUW

The movement is to universally impact women of all ages in whatever stage of life they are in, to overcome insecurities, adversities, and develop an unstoppable mindset. She Rises Studios educates, celebrates, and empowers women globally.

In this book, you will be inspired by a collaboration between She Rises Studios and 26 powerhouse-industry leading women from across the globe who will inspire purpose-driven women to STAND OUT, RISE, and THRIVE!

The book's mantra is "Collaboration OVER Competition."

Becoming An Unstoppable Woman Entrepreneur is written for women who are already in business as well as for women who are ready to launch themselves into the entrepreneurial world.

She Rises Studios offers:

- She Rises Studios Publishing
- She Rises Studios Public Relations
- She Rises Studios Podcast
- She Rises Studios Magazine
- Becoming An Unstoppable Woman TV Show
- She Rises Studios Community
- She Rises Studios Academy

Introduction

We won't stop encouraging women to be Unstoppable. This is just the beginning of our global movement.

She Rises, She Leads, She Lives...

With Love,

HANNA OLIVAS

ADRIANA LUNA CARLOS

SHE RISES STUDIOS

www.sherisesstudios.com

Adriana Luna Carlos

Co-Founder & CEO of She Rises Studios

Podcast & TV Host Personnel | Web & Graphic Designer | Best Selling Author | Women's Empowerment Coach | #BAUW Movement Creator

https://www.linkedin.com/company/she-rises-studios

https://www.instagram.com/sherisesstudios

https://www.facebook.com/sherisesstudios

https://www.sherisesstudios.com

Adriana Luna Carlos is a much sought-after expert in Web and Graphic design as well as a new Podcast and TV Host Personnel for She Rises Studios. For over 10 years she has embraced her passion in the digital arts field along with helping women worldwide overcome their insecure idiosyncrasies.

Today, when she's not spending time with her family and friends, you'll often find her helping women focus on rising up and becoming unafraid of success.

To learn more about Adriana Luna Carlos and how she can help you overcome obstacles in your business, mindset, or insecurities, visit www.SheRisesStudios.com

Young & Sassy!

by Adriana Luna Carlos

Some people may never realize just HOW MUCH I am in love with business. Not only that, but how I was born with an innate instinct to be an entrepreneur. I'll admit, I, like many before me, ignored some of the signs of my destiny to become a woman in business. In 2nd grade, I decided that I wanted to be a cardiologist and go to UCLA School of Medicine. I was accepted straight out of high school and I COULD NOT BELIEVE IT!!! I thought it was a fluke and that I didn't deserve the chance to go to my dream school. It was all that I had thought about and dreamt of for so long that it became my identity to my friends and family. But this is not the story of how I left my "dream" school and career, but rather a story of when I had my first entrepreneurial *success* and the lessons I learned along the way.

Surround Yourself With Like Minded Individuals

Growing up, I was very close to my younger cousin, Leslie, who is only a year younger than myself, and we were two peas in a pod. I considered us to be a Lucy and Ethel dynamic duo, though our nicknames for each other were "Choni" and "Màcalak." We were SILLY as can be, and I was always the ring leader because, back then, I was SASSY.

One day, we started noticing that lanyards were becoming a very popular trend among the kids in our school. We had this crazy idea of selling plastic lanyard strings, which were used to make custom and cutely designed lanyards in all shapes and sizes. I immediately got excited and inspired because, in my head, this was an opportunity to start our first business venture together. Once I pitched the idea to my cousin, she probably thought I was crazy, but regardless, she always had my back and was all in, and we became partners!

Implement A Solid Plan And Do Your Market Research

Our next steps were to get capital, because, as we all know, it takes money to make money. We needed to save up in order to invest in our product (being a spindle of plastic lanyard string). We were fortunate enough to have a grandfather who would often give us a dollar here and there to buy snacks. He didn't know that our intention was to save the money and buy our product; he just thought we wanted it for ourselves.

We hopped into our grandfather's mini-van and headed to Michael's Arts & Crafts store. The spindle ranged in price from $2.50 to $3.50, depending on the color and yardage included. We then started cutting up the string into 3 different lengths and priced them according to what we thought they could sell for (25¢, 50¢ and $1). (Keep in mind that we were only 8 to 9 years old, so we were doing a lot of guessing.) Then the next day at school, we had our products in a pencil box and opened shop during lunch on a picnic bench!

Expect Hiccups And Expand Your Team As You Grow

Our first day was a MASSIVE SUCCESS!!! We were so excited and definitely nervous about getting into any kind of trouble. As soon as one customer left, another would appear, and so on. Most of our business was based on kids spreading the information, aka the referral system. My cousin and I were riding the high that day of pure joy and excitement, and we could not believe that it was so easy! Or so we thought…

We quickly learned that we needed more manpower when some of our merchandise went missing! I remember my hot-tempered self being so mad, but I knew I couldn't do anything about it and that it was out of my control. My best friend at the time had always had problems with catching the bus home after school because she didn't have the money to do so. Quickly, the lightbulb went off in my head, and I offered her a job. I would pay her the amount she needed to take the bus in exchange for assisting us with sales or watching over our products. We were back in business, baby!!

Reinvest Some Of Your Profits & Upsell!

Now that we knew our product was good and that the demand and pricing points were successful, we wanted to scale our business. When we were back at the store the following week, we had our eye on our next product. It was a GLOW IN THE DARK version and we were SIKED. The spindle was twice as much, but we had so much saved up that we no longer had to rely on my grandfather for more capital. We cut up the strings, had our new price point in place, and the demand was there again. Groves of students would bombard us that day, and we felt sure we would get caught. Luckily, that was not the case.

We went back to my house that day and sat in the living room counting our profits. Giggling to ourselves, we didn't notice my dad was behind us. He quickly asked, "Where the heck did you guys get all that money?" We looked at each other and knew we were caught and there was no hiding it. Once we told our whole story to my dad, he started smiling and laughing and said, "You guys are so crazy!! I'm so proud of you! " When we realized he wasn't going to be mad, we told him all the details, and he was amazed more and more.

Protect Your Assets

Eventually, our luck ran out when someone decided to steal our box of lanyards. I then realized that you always have to be on alert and have safeguards in place. It's not just enough to hire additional employees, you have to have a system of checks and balances in place. These protocols will look different to every business model and company but are necessary to protect your assets.

So, why did I share this particular story with you? I really wanted to share some intimate memories and feelings of nostalgia, to help you understand and grasp my concept of entrepreneurship.

Although I was only about 8 to 9 years old, I learned so much in a short period of time. Also because I did not have bills to pay or anything to worry about, I got to truly enjoy the free spirit of entrepreneurship and all that it has to offer. There were no expectations or strings attached. We did it out of the love, passion, and the art of business.

I am passionate about the journey, the challenges, the psychology of business, helping people succeed, and feeling inspired by all the small to large successes. I am easily motivated because I learned at a young age how to filter out the negativity, and to harness and implement the positives.

I hope this story and chapter helps you to develop trust in yourself and your abilities. Learn to stay motivated and passionate and always remember your roots.

Takeaways

- If you fail, dust yourself off and get back to it.
- Listen to your instincts, put safeguards in place.
- There are many ways to make money with little to no investment, if you plan it out.
- Stay motivated, improve yourself and your products/services as you go
- Never run a business from a place of greed or selfishness.
- Being an entrepreneur is about having fun, finding your passion and overcoming unforeseen obstacles.

Hanna Olivas

Founder & CEO of She Rises Studios

Podcast & TV Host | Best Selling Author | Influential Speaker | Blood Cancer Advocate | #BAUW Movement Creator | Entrepreneur

https://www.linkedin.com/company/she-rises-studios

https://instagram.com/sherisesstudios

https://www.facebook.com/sherisesstudios

www.SheRisesStudios.com

Author, Speaker, and Founder. Hanna was born and raised in Las Vegas, Nevada, and has paved her way into becoming one of the most influential women of 2021. Hanna is the co-founder of She Rises Studios and the founder of the Brave & Beautiful Blood Cancer Foundation. Her journey started in 2017 when she was first diagnosed with Multiple Myeloma, an incurable blood cancer. Now more than ever her focus is to empower other women to become leaders because The Future is Female.

A Girl With A Dream

by Hanna Olivas

I've always known I wanted to be an entrepreneur, even before I could spell or say the word correctly. I had my first experience as a business owner at the mere age of 9 with my very own lemonade stand. I remember feeling so independent and from there it bloomed. My next venture was my own babysitting business. Mind you this was back in 1987, when life was what I consider much simpler than it is now.

As a teenager, I always had a passion for wanting to travel and for beauty. After high school, I left for California to pursue a career as a freelance makeup artist. It was then that I realized I didn't want to work for anyone but myself. However, I needed training in makeup, and training cost money. So, I worked as a waitress to pay for my schooling, to attend one of the best makeup academies on the west coast. Once I graduated, I began to work in the fashion and beauty industry. I traveled, worked with celebrities, and loved making women feel and look beautiful.

After 25 years in the industry and four children later, I felt I was missing out on my true calling and purpose. So, it was time to unplug and regroup in life. I opened a few different businesses, events, marketing, and back to owning my makeup line and shop. Although I still had this feeling, this void. I knew I loved working with women,

I loved helping others, what I didn't know was that it would lead me into opening She Rises Studios in the middle of a pandemic no less.

I always pictured myself on stage speaking to thousands of women but never knew why this was in my dreams or heart. I could hear the current crowd in my sleep clapping sometimes.

I know that sounds funny but it's true. One day I started Journaling and making a vision board and before I knew it, I had filled it with hundreds of goals and dreams.

One of them was to have my own TV show for women. I wanted to inspire women to be the best version of themselves. I believe that stems from some childhood trauma and me never feeling worthy enough, so if I could help other women from those feelings that's just what I wanted to do. Another dream or vision was to open a shelter for battered women and children. I wanted to help women heal. I began to see a pattern developing. How do I make this dream a reality? I asked myself that question over and over.

Finally, one day, I was sitting with my oldest daughter and it just hit me like a train. I told her, "we need to start a network for women!!." That is the day She Rises Studios was born. At first, it started with a simple Facebook and Instagram page filled with inspirational quotes that she or I had written.

I remember her and me sitting across from each other day in and day out trying to decide just what She Rises Studios was meant to do. We decided to step out in faith and host a podcast. Neither of us had any experience in podcasting, so we decided to take a class at our local library and the next thing we know, now we're podcast hosts for She Rises Studios Podcast!!

All I can say is wow! We invited women we knew to speak on topics and share their life experiences. It was also so exciting. Within the first three months, our podcast became syndicated. We were featured on all the major podcast platforms like Spotify, IHEART Radio, iTunes, and more.

We started with zero capital and a whole lot of faith. Now our podcast is one of the most sought out women's empowerment podcast shows in less than a year with no investment, no experience, just faith over fear, and a dream turned into reality. During all of this, we worked countless hours, made mistakes, lost sleep, shed tears, but through it all, we never gave up. We learned or we lost, but we never failed.

Now here comes the good part. Just six months into our podcast again sitting with my daughter I told her "we should write a book in collaboration with other like-minded women." I remember the look on her face, it kind of makes me laugh thinking about it now. She said, "what do you want the book to be about?" My answer was clear as day, Becoming An Unstoppable Woman because that's who we are.

We are unstoppable women who want to make a global impact together for all women.

Again, we had no experience, no capital, just a dream, and a vision. We began looking for like-minded women who would align with the book and the movement that we were creating.

The Becoming an Unstoppable Woman book and movement were born at the same time, created by two women who had a passion and purpose for entrepreneurship and community.

My dream didn't stop there. I began sharing our journey and story nationally and internationally. Our story gained traction, and we developed a global community of unstoppable women.

We released our first book on September 21st, 2021, titled "Becoming An Unstoppable Woman." The book hit 27 best-selling categories in 13 countries. I couldn't believe it until I held it in my very own hands. I remember the feeling of autographing my first book. It was such an extraordinary experience. One I will cherish forever! Now I am sitting here today writing my next book and chapter to you!

In less than 16 months She Rises Studios now has a podcast, TV show, Publishing company, Academy and we've expanded into the United Kingdom. I was just a girl with a dream and a passion. That dream became a reality. So, if you have a true desire to become an Entrepreneur, step out in faith, don't wait for the right time. Just do it, even if you have to do it afraid.

Yes, you may fall or hit some bumps in the road, but never lose sight of that dream. Keep going, growing, and learning. A true entrepreneur will never give up! Focus on the dream or goal until it becomes a reality. I strongly encourage you to sit and write it all out. Put in the action and the steps. Find a coach or mentor. Find and align with your She Tribe. Stay hyper-focused.

Throw away all your limiting beliefs and step out of your comfort zone. That is where the magic happens. Don't wait for the right opportunity or time, because truth be told, there isn't one.

We started in the middle of a worldwide pandemic with zero capital or investments. We worked our way up and never lost sight of the dream, not even for a second. Did I mention all of this was accomplished during my cancer diagnosis and treatment?

Against the odds, I stayed true to my dream. Through all the negative things and health issues, I chose to stand for my purpose and become an unstoppable woman entrepreneur! I hope you will find your Entrepreneur passion and run with it. Don't slow down, don't give up, live your life without limits. Trust the journey and process. Remember, it's always about progress, not perfection!

Love always,

Hanna

Michèle Kline

Kline Hospitality Consulting LLC,
Growth Consultant & Change Agent
https://www.linkedin.com/in/michelekline
https://www.instagram.com/michelekline khc
www.klinehospitality.com

Through intentionality and dedication, Argentinean immigrant Michèle Kline, built a career in the Hospitality Industry "playing chess and not checkers". In 2010, out of an unparalleled passion to improve service across the industry, she founded Kline Hospitality Consulting LLC, a successful firm focused on helping businesses and professionals grow. Michèle has repositioned some of the finest brands in the US and Latin America, including Fortune 500 ones. Her clients turn to her for help to transform their life, business, operating procedures, teams, communication style, upgrade time management skills and create thriving company cultures.

As a certified Coach and an operations process improvement expert, she is also known as "a fixer". Michèle is a respected Leader, whose focus is in building customer-focused Teams. With a strong background in Human Resources, in 2018 she was granted the Learning & Development Professional of the Year award by the Nevada Hotel & Lodging Association, apart from other recognitions throughout her career.

YOU are your biggest asset!

by Michèle Kline

Dear reader, I'm thrilled we meet again!!! If we actually haven't, welcome to my ride.

Now buckle up!

My name is Michèle and I am a quiet and humble Ninja Warrior of my own life. I am owner of "Kline Hospitality", where we help businesses and people grow by injecting quality and efficiency in everything they do. My industry? Hospitality.

As a Ninja Warrior, there are a few enemies I'm an expert in transforming. Wait! "Transforming"??? Why not "destroying", you must be thinking? Here is why. I am a lover (not a hater) and a strong believer that things should change and not just end.

You see, change is the greatest catalyst for growth. Now, meet my enemies: "Jackie Lousyservice", "Roberto Grumpyface", "Maxwell Financiallyanemic" and "Lavetta Weakleader".

Let me give you a wider perspective. I transform poor service quality into memorable experiences. Disengaged Teams into Teams who want to go the extra mile and never look to see what is on the other side of the fence. Underperforming operations start thriving and financial results, which were once a thing of the past, become the "talk of the town". Weak Leadership, my personal favorite, becomes motivational; stimulating; inspiring and most importantly, empathetic!

As an expert in process improvement, a magically fun training facilitator and developer of mind-blowing leaders, I have immeasurable passion for coaching businesses and people (individually as well) to become the best version of themselves. Believe me when I say, I can overwhelm you with my enthusiasm. BAM!

Are you excited yet?

You can certainly read more about my credentials, but for the sake of time, you will have to trust me as we embark on this journey together.

Now, how did I get started? Because in the end, we are here to talk about entrepreneurship. Did I always want to be "the owner"? Did I always know what I wanted? My purpose?

Not really.

A little bit of the backstory.

Just like many who created the path I did were catapulted by their disgust of "the Corporate world", I WAS NOT! I freaking LOVE the Corporate world, I am TOTALLY Corporate myself. What catapulted me to fly solo was poor leadership. To crown this state of mind, I felt uninspired. I was losing passion. The passion for my people, the passion for making a difference in the company's culture, for the details in every guest interaction, for exceeding expectations. That passion that has made me the professional I am today.

The trigger?

Over ten years ago, in a meeting with my boss and a group of professionals under my leadership, he decided to push a little too hard and SNAP!

My boss was an expert arrogant, who loved intimidation and taught me everything I shouldn't do as a Leader, including #metoo.

That day, in that meeting, he told us how ashamed he was. How our parents should be ashamed. How we would never be like him. He reminded us of the many cars, horses and cattle he owned. The many properties and money he had. What a bunch of losers we were and how WE WOULD NEVER BECOME ANYONE.

THIS was not corporate one bit!

After leaving that meeting while holding in tears of frustration, we all had to put on our "happy face" and hit the floor to ensure every guest at the hotel had "the most memorable experience". Not only did he not realize that you simply don't speak to ANYONE that way, he also failed to recognize that he was addressing the most revenue generating region, with the most profitability and best projection for growth out of the entire company.

WTF?! I'm thinking it too!

My Team was used to producing outstanding results, under pressure and with limited resources. How did we do it? We believed in the phrase "Teamwork makes the dream work!"

To make a long story short, as the empathetic Momma-Bear Leader that I am, I ended that evening in the office having everyone write on a piece of paper how they felt, I made them read it out loud and then each ran their paper through a shredder. Literally!

On my quiet drive home that night, I realized I had to change MY world if I wanted to change THE world.

Being a business owner is no easy task and not always the solution to your problems. Throughout the years, I have become aware that every business is different, but every business owner has the same common denominator: *we tend to forget that we are important to the business, far beyond the business being important to us.*

Here's a few tools to become an unstoppable entrepreneur without ever forgetting that YOU are your business' biggest asset:

⚒ **Harvest meaningful connections**. Don't just connect. Follow up, reach out, check in, lend a helping hand. Connect in a genuine way! The sale will eventually come.

⚒ **Find ways to collaborate**. Even though you are the owner, you don't have to do this on your own. Entrepreneurship can feel lonely at times. I have what I call my "toolbox" of service providers I tap into every time I see an opportunity to collaborate.

🀨 **Accept feedback** like a champ and apply it, use it, own it. Act. It's transformational when you look at it with perspective. Take it as free advice and set your emotions aside. It's business, it's not personal! (even when your business is your "baby"!)

🀨 **Learn to say "no"**. Think of yourself as a car. Cars have a reserve tank, you should have one too. Never let it go empty. There are times when you will be able to take on that project pro bono, speak at that conference and sit on that board. Learn to charge for your service when you have to and learn to manage your energy and time. Becoming overwhelmed does nothing for your business or brand.

Eleven years ago, I taught myself to work hard in silence and let success make the noise. I have built a business that allows me to spend quality time with my Family and enjoy life, while inspiring professionals to run their operations in a more meaningful and inclusive way. I am now able to impact more people, change more experiences and most importantly, make greater change! I am only able to do this by keeping in mind that I am important to my business.

Never ever forget that YOU are your biggest asset!

Michèle, a Ninja Warrior at heart.

Nicole Curtis

She Rise Studios| COO

https://www.linkedin.com/company/she-rises-studios

https://instagram.com/sherisesstudios

https://www.facebook.com/sherisesstudios

www.SheRisesStudios.com

Speaker, Author, and Coach. Nicole is a much sought-after expert with over 12 years of combined experience in Personal Growth and Self- Leadership Development which helped her overcome childhood sexual abuse, binge eating, and break free from toxic relationships. She founded Kapow Media LLC in 2018 and more recently became COO of She Rises Studios. When she's not enjoying the great outdoors or spending time with her family or with her fur and feathered friends, you'll often find her helping high-achieving women destroy their self-destructive thoughts, beliefs and behaviors so that they claim their God-given power and begin living life by their design.

Say Yes To being YOU!

by Nicole Curtis

Throughout my Entrepreneurial journey I have learned and done A LOT of things. I learned how to switch my mindset in order to lead myself, and how to plan, structure, and market my company. I have taught myself the ins and outs of utilizing social media platforms, and how to use them effectively. I've created online marketing and email campaigns, sales funnels, and developed strategy systems effectively. I learned to balance finances and how to manage my time efficiently. I've done 1:1 coaching, group coaching, and created courses and programs. I have taught workshops, master classes and challenges.

The list can go on but the #1 secret that I didn't know or learn that I know now when it comes to becoming an Unstoppable Woman Entrepreneur is just how important it is to first say YES to being YOU before anything else!!

I'm an ex-corporate executive who loved the game of climbing up the corporate ladder. The more I climbed up meant the more success and entitlement I would receive, and at the time those things were what mattered to me. I didn't care how I got success as long as I received it. What eventually ended up happening instead of feeling successful and living the dream life is I felt completely broken. Why? because while I was playing the game, I ended up losing myself in the process. Instead of feeling proud and accomplished I felt lonely and depressed. As I continued to climb, I got really good at wearing different masks. Masks that made me look successful, masks that made me look happy, masks that made me look like the true me but the woman wearing the masks actually was a completely different woman.

I truly believed that in order to reach success, there was no way it was going to be possible for me if I was going to be myself. I thought I had to become and pretend to be someone that I wasn't. I believed that if I was to be my true self it wouldn't be good enough, nor that I was worthy of it. Therefore, I copied and became a fake. I started my entrepreneurial journey out no different. I believed in order to be a successful woman entrepreneur I couldn't be me, so I copied other people and faked it in order to try to make it!

My first two and a half years as an entrepreneur was spent doing just that. I thought no one would take me seriously or look at me with any kind of respect, so I looked to the gurus to guide me. I assumed they knew better than I did, so I followed everything they said and taught to the T. This only made me anxious, stressed out, and burnt out more times than I could count. Until one day this girl became unstoppable, because I finally said yes to being me. I destroyed the masks and began showing up and running my company the way I wanted to!!!

Hun, let me just say this right here, your entrepreneurial journey needs to be your own! Grant yourself the permission and claim your power. Say yes to being you, and go change the world the way you want to!

Below are two major concepts that I use on a daily basis, so I never forget to say yes to being me, and always show up as my most powerful self in my company. My hope in sharing them with you is that you find them to be just as helpful as I have, while you are on your journey of becoming an Unstoppable Woman Entrepreneur.

Claim your God-given POWER!

Right now you have everything already inside of you to become an Unstoppable Woman Entrepreneur, you just haven't claimed it yet! You are perfectly and wonderfully made and the strengths, abilities, and talents that you have will always be enough!! There is no one on this planet like you that has the gifts that you have and the POWER you hold inside of you. When you say yes to you and you lead with a powerhouse mind in full trust and belief in yourself you won't only be unstoppable, you will be unmatchable in business!

How you design your business, the time and energy you choose to put into it, the kind of daily activities you do, the tools you use, the products you create, and the services you offer is all up to you! Stop wasting your time following the "gurus", taking every course you see online, and opt into every freebie you see. Stop getting distracted by the next shiny thing while spending countless hours searching online trying to find the answer for success. Just start "being you", show up in your company following your soul, heart, and intuition with full trust, belief and faith, alternately your POWER, because that is where true company success comes from!!

Establish Company Principles!

When I started the process of destroying the fake me and began showing up as my most powerful self in my company, I created a list of what I call company principles. My company principles are the fundamental piece to running a successful company. They are used as a guide to help keep me focused, aligned and intentional inside my company! Anytime I feel weary, uncertain, fearful, doubtful, and/or unworthy I go to my principles. Anytime I am dreaming, envisioning, growing and evolving I go back to those principles.

Today I challenge you to create your own company principles and read and follow them every day, because I know they will help you say yes to being you in your journey of becoming an Unstoppable Woman Entrepreneur!

Below are a few examples of mine for you to see.

- I may not have the answer now but I will trust that it will be revealed to me when I'm ready to receive it!

- I am worthy of receiving the blessing that comes my way each and every day!

- With God I am an Unstoppable Woman!

- I am capable of achieving greatness!

Here at She Rises Studios we empower, inspire and support women all around the world through our free and paid services. If you want help in claiming your POWER, becoming Unstoppable, and leveling up in your life and business then visit www.sherisestudios.com.

Alicia Marcos Birong

ChatterGIrls INC. & Guided Choices. Pioneer in Pediatric Hypnotherapy and Life Coaching. Owner and Founder of After School Program (ChatterGIrls) and Pediatric Life Coach Certification Programs

https://www.linkedin.com/in/alicia-marcos-birong-4716177
https://www.instagram.com/guided_choices
https://www.facebook.com/guidedchoices
https://www.guidedchoices.org/pediatric-life-coaching
https://www.guidedchoices.org
https://chattergirls.net

Alicia Marcos Birong is a pioneer in the field of child mindfulness, speaking on the same stages with Mother Teresa and Pope John Paul II.

As the founder of Guided Choices, Alicia's signature programs have gathered national attention for their transformative abilities of children.

ChatterGirls™ offers in-person, hands-on guidance for 8-14 year old girls. Pediatric Life Coaching™ instructs parents, teachers, and coaches how to effectively help children overcome their daily hurdles.

Alicia's best selling book "Changing the Chatter" assists young girls in developing life skills for becoming strong, confident women.

A recipient of McHenry County Hero's Award, Alicia's passion for empowering children is evident. With 25+ years of experience as a therapist, counselor, life coach, and hypnotherapist, Alicia shares her expertise with communities across the country. You may have seen her on national television or working alongside companies such as Coca-Cola, Girls Scouts of America, American Express, and the YWCA.

Changing the Chatter

by Alicia Marcos Birong

You're too ugly. You're too shy. You're too fat. You're not good enough. These are the words that so many people tell themselves day in and day out. As adults, it's hard to break out of the negativity in our minds. That negativity is what I call Chatter. It's the tiny voice in your head that just won't keep quiet. Whenever you have a moment to celebrate or a moment of pride, that chatter wants to pop back up and say hello in the worst ways possible.

As women, we've had to endure a lot. We've been ignored and we've had to work harder to be heard. When we're paid less than men, the chatter may tell us we're not as worthy, which couldn't be further from the truth.

What is the truth? Everyone has chatter and everyone can change the chatter. The second truth is that the journey to change the chatter needs to begin in childhood. That is when our minds are most susceptible to the negative chatter. We're trying to fit in. We're making friends and understanding our own personalities. Our individual quirks are beginning to stand out more. Parts of our bodies are changing, some for the better. Some, not so much.

After years of listening and working with women and children, I could recognize patterns. Those in control of the chatter found ways to help themselves. Those without control ended up carrying it around with them when they're 35, 45, or even 65 years old.

I recognized it because I was one of those women. The issues of unworthiness, low self-esteem, lack of value, and shallow self-confidence were all issues I faced as a child, and it continued throughout my adulthood. I know now that I went through all of those painful years in order to see both sides of my life. Looking back gives me perspective on the type of person I never want any girl to turn into. Looking forward gives me hope that the empowered girl has never been more recognized.

All of that negative chatter in our minds is not the truth. We need to change the chatter. But how?

Self-esteem is developed in a young girl from around 8 to 14 years old. That's when most of the negative chatter will pop up. So, if we could change the chatter at that age, just imagine the change in dynamic in what their life would be like at 35!

In order to be successful in life, girls need to be able to believe in themselves and their abilities. Sometimes, like in my case, it takes another person to point out why you are so great. So, I combined all of the tools from 30 years of work in counseling, therapy, and coaching to create a program built specifically around the challenges I faced growing up. The program became ChatterGirls.

I had never really considered myself an entrepreneur until the first day of ChatterGirls. It was then I realized that my journey would be so much different compared to anything else I had experienced in the many roles in my life. It's one thing to help others. It's a completely different mindset to take what you've experienced personally, develop it into a program, and provide a path forward for the women of tomorrow.

What's been most exciting for me through this experience is all of the changes. As a creator, what you begin with never looks like the current version. What started as a small circle of 10 girls has blossomed into a national program hosted by afterschool programs and parents' groups. I'm no longer running every program. It's spreading so more girls can be empowered.

Past ChatterGirls are now in high school, or college, or starting their own families. They come back and assist the girls coming into the program after them. They can share their experiences and the girls in the program just look up to them so much. It's one thing to have an adult run the program, but when girls only 5 years older come back, it creates a whole new connection and dynamic.

The program is fun. It's creative and allows the girls to show off their own creativity. They have time to share with one another, but also time to journal and focus on their own thoughts independently, in a positive way. We celebrate them and their uniqueness in every part of the program.

C.H.A.T.T.E.R.

Celebrate. Celebrate your life every day.

Happy. Finding reasons to be happy.

Aspire. Aspiring to be open more.

Truthful. No matter the price, truthfulness is the way.

Thoughtful. Your life grows when you think of others beyond yourself.

Empowered. Look within yourself and know you have everything within you.

Responsible. It's your responsibility to yourself and others to commit to all of the above.

Being an entrepreneur is scary. It's takes changes and admitting when you're wrong. Growing is as much about listening and watching, and making changes as it is about content creation, sales numbers, and marketing techniques. These were all areas I had to learn, with a lot of time spent second guessing decisions. Anytime I second guess a decision, I can look to the girls and to the program to keep me on track. After all, I was the very first ChatterGirl, and it's always good to have a refresher.

To the generations that come behind the current groups of girls, you have a head start and you can make this even better.

To the girl who can not speak during the first day of the program, you will find your voice. You will have the last word. I've seen it firsthand with so many others like you. A girl just like you became the performing lead at her school play.

To the girl who doesn't have the confidence (yet) to try something new, no one is perfect when they begin. I've witnessed girls grow beyond any of their expectations.

To the girl who can't see herself as a leader (yet), I watched one of our very first girls take what she learned, apply it to high school life, and write about it for her college entrance exam.

To the girl who cries and is having a hard time dealing with autism, you too are special and have abilities that make you wonderfully unique. There was a girl just like you who grew so much she was able to approach opportunities to speak in front of the entire church.

To the girl who doesn't feel like she fits in or has a place, there's always an open seat waiting for you. ChatterGirls is always for you.

And you.

And you.

It took others to believe in me, and because of them I learned to believe in myself. Because I was able to believe in myself, I can now see the smiles on the faces of so many girls who realized they could be whoever they want to be.

ChatterGirls are the ones who face the chatter straight on and change it. They do not accept others' negative remarks. They are the ones who find their place on the playground, assisting the girl who once bullied them. They are the hockey players who kept on playing. They are the girls with dyslexia who were telling themselves they could never become a writer.

If you know a girl (or you were the girl) who has a hard time changing the chatter, reach out to me. We have programs all across the country. We have former ChatterGirls who can share their personal stories.

I too was a ChatterGirl. To be able to say I'm an author, entrepreneur, writer, coach, mother, and grandmother is something that never would've happened…

had I continued to believe the negative chatter in my head.

Charly Niesen

Recovery Specialist

Child Protection Advocate

Mental Health Practitioners

"You're so busy doubting yourself while so many are intimidated by your potential." -author unknown

Charly Rose Niesen may not be your typical entrepreneur, in fact typical does not even come close to describing this unstoppable woman who lives in the Brainerd Lakes Area in central Minnesota. Her story of recovery gives hope to the masses, and her strength and courage are un-measurable. Charly is a changemaker, a fierce advocate, supportive wife and mother of seven children ages 3 to 21 years of age. One of her values is sisterhood and knows from personal experience the importance of surrounding herself with passionate people who continue to challenge her to step out of her comfort zone and continue to grow into a more authentic version of herself. Celebrating over 15 years clean from methamphetamine, Charly is a mental health practitioner, recovery support specialist, WRAP facilitator and child protection advocate. She is one who has never given up, she is an opportunist, has taken what people would call failures and has used those moments to create new opportunities. When she has downtime she enjoys her husband's cooking, watching the Vikings play and spending time with her children and husband looking for Lake Superior agates on the North Shore.

I am Charly

by Charly Niesen

I'm a lifestyle entrepreneur. Growing up I thought I had a NORMAL childhood, however, I soon realized that my normal looked different from all my friends. By the time I was 15 years old, my dad had been in 12 treatment centers for his addiction to narcotics. At one family group session, my dad's counselor looked right at me and said, "Charly, I see so much of your dad in you."

At that time, I thought he was complimenting me; however, I would soon realize that he meant I would struggle with addiction. I began skipping school, stealing cars, and running away from home. I was in juvenile detention centers, on probation, and even had to complete a 120-day boot camp. At this point in my life, I had dropped out of school in the 9th grade and was what many called "defiant and rebellious". I was afraid, lost, and just trying to find my place in all the chaos.

At age 17, I was placed in a detention center, and it was there that I found out I was pregnant with my first child. I didn't have to go far to inform his father as he was right next door at the jail annex. I wanted to be the best mother I could be, so I started taking parenting classes, secured a job, and took classes towards obtaining my GED.

On July 19, 2000, I gave birth to my first son. Holding my perfect newborn son, my heart filled with a love I like I never felt before. I found out my baby's father was cheating on me and had left me days before I gave birth. After leaving the hospital, with my parents' help, I moved into my own apartment with my son.

One night, I received a call in the middle of the night from my baby's father asking, "Can I come see my son?" It was the moment I had prayed for, seeing him holding our son. This pattern continued for a month before I said, "Dustin it's 3 AM, I am tired and have zero energy." He talked me into letting him stay the night, and that's when I was introduced to methamphetamine.

Dustin told me it would help me feel energized and lose the baby weight. Within weeks, I had lost the baby weight. I also lost my job, my apartment, and my son. Dustin ended up in jail for domestic abuse. I was homeless and asked Dustin's mother to take our son until I got on my feet and healthy. I didn't think it would take me six years.

Dustin and I parted ways and I found myself in another unhealthy relationship. My meth use went from snorting to IV use. I was a full-blown addict and used heroin daily. My addiction also resulted in legal implications. I was picked up on a warrant and was sentenced to eight months in jail, where I found out I was pregnant again.

For the next 18 months I remained sober, taking classes, going to therapy, working, and meeting with many professionals every week, with the goal of reunification with my children. <u>(I am very proud to say with all my pregnancies, I never used any drugs or alcohol.)</u>

During the final stages of my child protection case, I found out I was expecting again. That is when I was introduced to Kimberly.

Kimberly's presence stopped people in their tracks during a meeting when she slammed her hands on the table making everyone jump and look at her. She said, "You know what the problem is here, I think everyone forgot to tell Charly how magnificent she is." From that day forward I sat up just a little bit taller and am forever grateful to her that she didn't judge me by labels on a piece of paper. She saw me for who I was and could be and loved me when I couldn't love myself.

Soon after I gave birth to my beautiful daughter, I was informed I had to leave the hospital without her and that I would hear from my child protection worker. Eventually, I went to a family foster home with my daughter. I agreed to sign my parental rights over for my son after I was told if I didn't, I would risk losing them both. It took me 20 minutes to sign the necessary forms, with tears streaming down my face looking down at my daughter. I wish I could say this is the part where I became my authentic self. Unfortunately, my depression started to set in once I realized that my children would not grow up together.

For the next six months, I used daily. I missed my court date, and my parental rights were involuntarily terminated. I was too afraid to take my own life, yet I was too afraid to live. During this time, I met Brandon, my husband. On Feb 12, 2006, we decided to get clean. Three months into our sobriety I found out we were expecting our first child together., Brandon held my hand and said, "I promise to be the best father." Sixteen years later and with three more children, he has kept that promise.

A year into my recovery, Kimberly and I stood on a mountain top, and she asked me, "Who are you?" I meekly said, "Charly". She asked again, and in that moment, I found my voice and shouted, "I AM CHARLY".

I obtained GED and went to college. I began working at a local mental health center using my lived experiences to mentor and support others. I became a Mental Health Practitioner, Child Protection Mentor, Recovery Specialist, WRAP facilitator, Life Coach, and public speaker with current goals of creating my own non-profit. I volunteer with BLADE, a community awareness program for drug education and prevention. I work closely with Meta 5, the program that turned my life around. My experiences opened so many doors and helped me to support others in breaking the stigma of substance use and mental health. I work at the same treatment program I got sober. I continue to advocate to break the stigma that held me back for so long.

Pamela Kurt

Best Version of You LLC

Professional Women Coach

https://www.linkedin.com/in/pamela-kurt-41a26ba

https://www.facebook.com/Best-Version-You-103772311530954

www.BestVersionYou.com

www.PamKurt.com

Ms. Kurt as an attorney and business owner have won many awards and honors as well as held multiple Leadership Roles in her community. She has found a new passion. Her passion is to support and to empower women to be the best they can!

The most personal enjoyment is when her clients find their own way. Ms. Kurt has also a private professional women life coaching practice. BE THE BEST VERSION of YOU! This is an opportunity to elevate professional women to be the best version of themselves. Dream, Believe and Achieve is her signature coaching program. Her coaching program has allowed her clients on a powerful self-discovery journey. She is currently accepting new private coaching clients. Please contact her at BestVersionYou.com to start your journey to become the BEST YOU.

What Being An Entrepreneur Means To Me

by Pamela Kurt

What being an entrepreneur is to me.

An entrepreneur has a certain mindset. This is the key to get through the journey. What are those basic qualities and the mindset to enable people to identify and make the most of opportunities while helping people be their best self?

How do you get there? This is how I got there and am still moving forward!

Faith, Family, Perseverance, and Resilience.

Faith. I work without a net as I have said many times. My safety net is GOD! I don't have a rich family or a rich husband. I have been so blessed because I have been able to open my heart and mind to God and make the next steps faithfully through my life and transitions but sometimes, you think you hear something and it's not the right direction. Be mindful and let it happen and try to remain prayerful in the "next steps". As a single mom and trying to work and go to college, I needed a lot of faith. Times were very scary. It took years to fully trust.

There was one time I was selling a car, a 1988 Chevy Cavalier. It was a standard (stick shift). I had just bought an automatic thinking easier with the baby etc. Well, a lady called and asked about the car and I explained the mileage, condition and that's it's a standard and we discussed how it would be a great first car for her daughter. The daughter could learn on a standard and how great that was for her daughter to learn this skill and we negotiated a price. I went and got the title notarized and was waiting that evening for the lady and her daughter to arrive. She called and stated the daughter doesn't want to learn standard and she was sorry but she wasn't going to be purchasing the car.

This was early on in my journey when I knew everything and way before I went back to college. I was clueless about a lot of things and literally went off on her. "I spent my day getting the title notarized now what? I have to get a replacement title and all of that costs money…blah blah blah." The lady graciously offered to pay for the replacement title and I of course with ego and pride, was gruff and I declined. I cooled off and just waited.

A few days later someone called about the car. When talking I was immediately on guard and explained it is a "standard". The guy stated, "Of course that's what I was looking for as a work car." He wanted to come see it tomorrow. Of course, I needed to sell it and agreed. He offered me FULL PRICE! There weren't any negotiations etc. and I still had the title I had already started for the prior transfer so it was ready to go. Since he offered FULL PRICE, I actually earned about $600 more than I was settling for with the first lady. At that moment, I learned GOD's time. I have to be faithful.

I have tried to use that lesson in many business decisions. If it doesn't work or feel right, it's not right and to have faith something bigger and/or better is coming. I have learned that if I am faithful not only the right decision will come, but God provides.

Are you faithful to God and yourself to listen for the right opportunities? Faithful enough to have the patience to get to the next level? Faithful enough to take the chances? Faith can be scary but it's worth it.

Family. My family are workers! My parental side were innovators, farmers, and factory workers. While they ran their farm, they also worked full time. God set me up for entrepreneurship with both sides. My Maternal side grandparents also owned their own business, a car lot, and worked many side jobs to make it and get where they needed to be. My father himself owned his own dump truck business. Sometimes, I just know things. How people are going to respond. How to market things and help others. I am grateful for the God given gifts from my family. It runs in my blood. I remember fundraising and doing events as early as grade school from setting up booths to sell corn from the farm and into high school. Both sets of my grandparents and my father are now gone but wow what lessons! I am ever so grateful for them.

I still try to do the things they did and show an example to the next generation. My son started his own business, a production company that creates short movies. My nieces each are always selling things and starting their own businesses. I hope I can leave and show them the innate abilities to continue the entrepreneurial spirit. Some may say I am a serial entrepreneur. This means I own/run multiple businesses. I love it and it serves the passion and purpose I am meant for.

Perseverance. Don't Quit. Determination. Believe in yourself. With God all things are possible, BUT YOU HAVE TO DO THE WORK. Sometimes the road is long and the end isn't in site but if you can dream it, you can have it. It was brought to your mind and put on your heart for a reason. We have all heard these quotes and cliches before. As you go through this process, be kind and take care of you. This was another lesson I had to learn.

I thought perseverance was the grind and hard work daily! If I didn't work 18 hours in a day and physical hurt, I wasn't working hard enough. Not necessarily. Keep your focus and be open. Your perseverance will be rewarded. You can do this and note each path is different for each of us. God will lead your path and the way. Working for yourself and being an entrepreneur can have many challenges, as we experienced in COVID but there are also many benefits. Just don't quit.

Many of life's failures are people who did not realize how close they were to success when they gave up. -Thomas Edison

Don't give up. If it's on your heart, it's there for a reason. Don't beat yourself up and don't quit. Sometimes we need that reminder. Again and again.

Resilience. This is the last piece to my formula. I do make mistakes and wrong choices. You bounce back. You can always find ways to replace money but stay true to yourself and the relationship you make. As I mentioned, COVID was hard on most entrepreneurs. Yes, there was some relief out there, but it also gave a lot of time to reevaluate and bounce back. Many of us were able to review some of the things in our business and see if it was still a fit. Many of us found more resourceful and different ways to complete the task and challenges. Life happens but know you can and will BOUNCE back with the right support.

Everyone has their own formula to be a successful entrepreneur. For me, my formula is *Faith, Family, Perseverance, and Resilience*. I don't doubt you are on the right path. I am happy to help you get there. This is why I started the coaching business. I want to help others find their formula. We all have different paths and I am honored when I can help others fulfill their dreams and be the entrepreneur they are meant to be.

Be the Best YOU!

Lovely LaGuerre

Founder Pure Heavenly Hair Boutique

https://www.linkedin.com/company/pure-heavenly-hair

https://instagram.com/pureheavenlyhair

https://m.facebook.com/Pure-Heavenly-Hair-Boutique-107278091130735

www.PureHeavenlyHair.com

www.LovelySellsVegas.com

Lovely LaGuerre is a Serial Entrepreneur and Amazon International Bestselling Author. She shares her story that will empower you, will inspire you, and will uplift you. She believes in the power of collaborating with other women and sees how it lends to the growth of all involved. Lovely is a successful Commercial and Luxury Real Estate Agent. She is on a mission to help others turn their real estate investment dreams into a reality. She's also the Founder of Pure Heavenly Hair Boutique, and her Luxury Beauty brand transforming, inspiring, and empowering women to unleash their beauty inside and out. She is a member of NAIOP, CALV, NAR, GLVAR Association, Wealthy Women Inner Circle, Becoming An Unstoppable Woman, and many more.

Conquering My Journey

by Lovely LaGuerre

My journey as an entrepreneur started as soon as I desired to create something. I have always wanted to leave a mark throughout my life, something that has never happened before, something that would be electric.

As a child, I always had my room filled with unique objects that no one else had. I was a collector of sorts, always looking for more to add to my collection.

As a teen, I was not the normal teen spending time with friends and going out having fun every night after school. At a young age most of my time was used by planning my future and figuring out ways to make it better. No one understood me, but I found comfort in being who I was very young. No matter how much my friends tried to change me, I would not budge.

I knew every single step that I needed to take for me to get where I wanted. Time passed, and I started working on my first business idea and got some success. It seemed like a breeze until the day came when I realized that maybe it was not what I wanted anymore.

Every successful individual has miscarried at some point, but instead of giving up, they pick themselves up and try again. This is the only way to survive in this world where everything else seems to be against you.

Well... that's the number one lesson I have learned over the years failure will come your way, but instead of running away from it, embrace it. If you do that, then you are one step closer to success.

I believe in the power of writing. Whenever I sit down to write, my mind becomes clear and focused. This is not just for me but for anyone who desires to create something amazing. Writing makes any goal achievable because you have a path clearly defined before you, all you must do is follow it.

When it comes to emotional contemplation and planning, I recall staying up late many nights scribbling down my next actions. Endless restless nights and restless days followed, and I was stumped as to how to fit the puzzle pieces together. I would not gotten this far if I had not planned and written down my thoughts. I analyze every aspect of my life, and now I can see the results.

I am always on the lookout for new ways to improve myself, and my brain is continuously at work, trying to figure out the perfect formula of success. My main source of inspiration comes from biographies; I love reading them since it simply reminds me that everything is conceivable if you put your heart and soul into it. No matter how many times you get hit down, stand up and try again. The only way someone learns from their mistakes is by going through it repeatedly until they get it right.

As I began to move into my position as an entrepreneur, I had to realize that my life had changed. It took me some time to fine-tune and follow this new path I had created for myself, but everything fell into place once I got the hang of it. There were days when I had to work twenty-four hours straight; there were others where I was worn out that all I could do was lay in bed the next morning.

I had to realize that I am no longer just an individual, that now I have to consider the people around me and their needs. Nothing is more important than family and friends; I had to adjust my vision of the world and turn it into something bigger.

My life as an entrepreneur has taught me that I should never limit myself or my abilities. There are no boundaries for success; one has to break boundaries and go beyond what is expected. My ambitions are always to strive for more. I want to become an example of success for those who don't believe in themselves.

I want to keep going until my last breath and inspire all those around me. This is not just about making a few bucks but also about changing the world. I want to be remembered as someone who wanted to make a difference in this world or at least made an effort to do so.

When I first came into entrepreneurship, my visions grew exponentially to a growth mindset, rather than a day to day mindset. Entrepreneurs are free to live their lives on their terms. Yes, there are restrictions and rules, but once you are successful enough, you are the one who sets them. You are in control of your whole life, and the only person who can limit you is yourself. I learned that the world is my oyster and that the limits only exist in my head.

I believe that a powerful mind is the key to success throughout my journey. If you have your thoughts structured perfectly, then achieving anything becomes possible. You need to know what you want and how exactly to go about it. When you put all these together and execute them perfectly, then no one can stop you from achieving anything.

As an entrepreneur, I have faced many difficulties in my life, but with the right amount of perseverance, I succeeded. Once you accept yourself by researching and gaining knowledge, you become unstoppable.

Giving up is not a choice when you are in this business. You need to stay ahead of the game, even if it means working long hours and sometimes even during holidays.

To become an unstoppable woman and entrepreneur, you must first understand who you are and constantly be aware of what you have agreed to. When it comes to serious thought and preparation, I recall staying up late many nights scribbling down my next actions. I thought about all the possible scenarios, even the highly unlikely ones. It was important for me to make long-term plans and establish my goals. Once I was clear about what I wanted, my success followed.

It all becomes clear, and you see the bigger picture at some point. When you see the bigger

picture, nothing will ever stop you from achieving your goals.

You can do anything you put your mind to. It takes a lot of time and hard work to grow and develop a healthy positive mindset and to see beyond the possibilities. Accomplishing an

innovative mindset as an entrepreneur consists of various beliefs, goals, ideas, and thought

processes that ultimately can contribute to the business owner mindset.

You must dedicate your life to what you want, so go out there and give it your all!

Remember along the way to always be Kind!

Krystal Vernee'

Simply SHE LLC

CEO

http://www.linkedin.com/in/krystalvernee

http://www.instagram.com/i_simply_she

http://www.facebook.com/isimplyshe

http://www.isimplyshe.com

http://www.krystalvernee.com

Krystal Vernee' is a serial womenpreneur, author, speaker, business coach and brand strategist. She owns Divas & Dolls Fitness, a pole and sensual dance studio; Cirque Sensual, a sensual aerial dance brand; Simply SHE, a coaching business and podcast and Krystal Vernee' is her personal brand. An engineer by trade, Krystal knew that entrepreneurship was the ultimate goal early in her professional career. She has always been passionate about empowering women, creating a safe space for them to unapologetically be themselves and providing the support they need to make the transformation their passion into profits. Krystal encourages others to tap into her zone of genius through the Simply SHE Podcast and her coaching program: The Brand BuildHER BlueprintTM. She teaches womenpreneurs to gain clarity and confidence in their brand so that they can build a 6 figure plus business through strategy and systems.

Build Your Brand Like A Boss

by Krystal Vernee'

Entrepreneurship is one of the most difficult challenges that I have ever faced but, if you know me, you know I absolutely love a challenge. I truly believe that it is in the most difficult times, our lowest points, enduring our greatest struggles coupled with how we choose to handle those moments that define our character. In the words of Coco Chanel, "Keep your heels, head and standards high". I have always strived for excellence and have never lowered my aims, even in the most difficult times. As I am writing this chapter, I am a serial womenpreneur with four businesses, each of them distinctly branded. I am a pole and sensual dance studio owner, aerial studio owner, business coach, podcaster, speaker, best-selling author, and brand strategist. Do you have to have multiple businesses to be an "Unstoppable Woman Entrepreneur"? No, not at all. However, you must have drive, determination, grit, guts, and the will to never give up. You must develop what I like to call an architect or a builder's mentality, constantly constructing, making, creating, and bringing your vision to life. Not everyone will be able to see you as "The Boss" or see the vision for your business, but remember this: God gave you the vision, He didn't give it to them.

Anyone can start a business, but building a brand takes time and unstoppable effort. It takes hard work, dedication, strategy, becoming a student of the game, confidence in your decisions and a strong sense of self. Becoming an Unstoppable Woman Entrepreneur is not only about having a profitable business, it is also having the ability to leave a legacy and building a brand that precedes you. As a business coach and brand strategist, I tell my clients to "Build Your Brand Like A Boss" so that your brand literally takes on a life of its own. It becomes organic, magnetic and evolves. Building your brand like a boss teaches you to hustle until you no longer have to introduce yourself and I can show you how.

Like most new entrepreneurs, I struggled my first few years in business. I was trying to find my footing, getting my branding together, deciding what I wanted to offer, trying to figure out the marketing, etc. I put in blood, sweat, tears, countless investments, you name it. I wanted to quit 1,000 times but then I also couldn't live without it. As I look back on that time in my life, I was constantly seeking approval and confirmation that what I was doing was right instead of trusting my own judgement. I was seeking approval from really anyone to show that I was on the "right" path. While most people smiled and told me what I was doing was "cool", I could tell they really didn't care or understand. It was then that I realized, they couldn't see the vision and I had to empower myself to be confident enough to run my business.

Once I fully accepted who I was and who I was becoming, my business flourished. I started 3 more businesses 5 years after opening my studio and I haven't looked back. I was even able to make connections between all my brands and how they aligned with my purpose to empower women. I am extremely passionate about branding because I believe it is what separates you from your competition, it grows your community, and it develops lifelong customers that are your biggest ambassadors. Each brand that I built follows the same formula and it is what I teach my clients because your brand is the soul of your business. If you want to *Build Your Brand Like A Boss,* you should follow these steps:

1. **Develop a strong sense of self.** You are the brand, whether you like it or not. Knowing who you are, what you stand for and what's important to you will make it that much easier to establish your brand values and operate with integrity.

2. **Hire a coach.** Free content will only take you so far and you cannot reverse engineer what you can't see. I'm not just saying that because I am a coach, but it makes all the difference in the world in your business. Having someone that's been where you're trying to go can literally take years off the time it takes you to scale your business. To put things in perspective, I have a coach and will continue to have coaches and mentors to help me get to where I want to be.

3. **Develop a strategy.** Do not use the spaghetti method. Everything should be done intentionally and have a purpose. Listen to your brand community (your target market) and be sure that what you offer truly does serve them.

4. **Learn to love the word "no".** There will be many opportunities, but all will not be a good fit for your business. You must be a strong visionary and know what makes logical sense for your brand, your niche, and what could be seemingly easy money that will end up costing you more in the long run.

5. **Stay consistent.** While you may not see the results you seek at first, you must show-up consistently for your brand. This not only includes where but how you show up. Choose where you will

show-up for your brand community, what you will offer and how you will help them get results. Constantly changing your product suite, where you market your business and how it will help your ideal client becomes confusing for both you and them. Consistency is key to sustainability.

While entrepreneurship has been one of my most difficult experiences, it has also been one of the most rewarding. I have the privilege of touching the lives of so many women through sensual dance and aerial arts, podcasting, business coaching programs, speaking engagements, books and so much more. I didn't become an unstoppable woman entrepreneur overnight, it was a process and a journey, one that I am still on. I hope this chapter has provided some insight into the world of entrepreneurship and motivation for you to keep going. For more business and branding tips or to find out how you can work with me to build your brand, visit my website listed in my bio. May you go forth and *Build Your Brand Like A Boss*.

Aileen V. Sicat

Lawyer | Educator | Writer | Spiritual Life Coach

https://www.linkedin.com/in/aileens

http://www.instagram.com/sheisaileens

https://rainbowswithaileen.com

Aileen V. Sicat is a Spiritual Life Coach and Tarot Coach. She also gets to be a lawyer, educator, writer, speaker. Without realizing it, she has always been coaching and motivating the people around her even as she wears her lawyer and educator hats.

Aileen knows how it is to have many different passions in life and the challenges that come with reinventing oneself. She herself has shifted gears several times. She also understands how some would prefer to have coaching/reading sessions via text chat or audio call rather than face to face or via video call.

Today, Aileen aims to empower people from all walks of life all over the world and to accompany them in their journey to pursue the best life for themselves. To learn more about her, connect with her via Instagram, LinkedIn or through her website.

Turning Passion into Purpose

by Aileen V. Sicat

Many of us have at one point dreamt of being an entrepreneur. The idea is to hold our own hours, to call the shots and be our own boss. Is it as simple as that? Of course not. Nothing ever is. The base is dirty even while the superstructure may seem attractive. Then again, just because it is not easy-peasy does not mean we have to give up without trying.

You and I

I graduated with a business course in college. Did I start my own entrepreneurial venture right after graduation? No. Did I work for an employer first to learn the ropes and get ideas? Uh-uh. Instead, I went to law school. After that, I worked in a law office and then became a law professor. Sure, I pursued graduate studies. Was it an MBA? Not quite. I opted for a Master of Arts and then a Master of Laws.

Outwardly it may seem that I set aside any plans that has to do with business but it was just always looming in the horizon and waiting for the right time. As I write this, I cannot claim to be an established entrepreneur. In fact, I am still on the starting stage and feeling my way through things. So why am I writing this and why are you reading this again?

It's because I sense you are a little like me and may even see yourself in my own experiences. Though no two experiences are exactly alike, we may be traveling parallel paths. Even with different contexts, our concerns as starting out/aspiring entrepreneurs may be almost the same. Even if you see yourself as an established entrepreneur or as a person who does not aspire to be one, you may still have an interest in seeing people like me navigate this world of entrepreneurship and perhaps even give us a boost in your own way.

Double-edged Sword

Starting from scratch and in my case, as basically a one-woman team, is not easy. True, I get to call the shots. It is my vision that will be implemented. On the other hand, I am also the one that is going to finance whatever expenses are entailed to bring that vision to life.

Yes, I will hold my hours and work when I want to. Then again, what income is expected for the lazy and intermittent worker?

There are privileges and then there are responsibilities. The two go hand in hand. There are risks but yes, we can turn them into calculated risks by doing our research and by consulting experts and experienced individuals. On the opposite side of risks, there are also potential rewards waiting on the other end.

Deciding to be an entrepreneur for me means embracing the double-edged nature of things and being at peace with it. There are pros and there are cons. In my opinion, the pros outweigh the cons as do the potential rewards outweigh any risks.

Mixing Business with Pleasure

Growing up, I heard many times that we should not mix business with pleasure. I have always wondered why not? When we love what we are doing, it never feels like a chore. Instead, each day is brand new and an adventure. When it comes to entrepreneurship, I am a firm believer that I should pursue something related to my passions and advocacies. I need to feel that I am not just earning a living but also somehow giving back and providing value in ways I feel most comfortable with.

I am most comfortable when I feel I have empowered other women to pursue the path they choose for themselves. Motivating people and accompanying them in their journey as they probe their own thoughts and feelings and make choices feeds my soul. For these reasons, I decided to start my own spiritual life coaching business. I also do card coaching (not just readings) and offer other intuitive services including reiki.

I chose this path not just because I am passionate about spiritual work, card readings and energy healing. It is also because I feel I can impact many lives and be there for people who may need me in their journey. This is also something I can do for people who are thousands of miles away from me with the use of technology. We can do it via video, audio, email, text chat even. Physical distance and pandemics do not prevent anything.

With this choice, I hope to be able to mix business with pleasure in a most harmonious manner. I aim to turn passion into purpose.

Taking the Plunge

As I said earlier, I am in the early stages of being an honest to goodness unstoppable entrepreneur. I used to do coaching and readings sporadically or for friends or friends of friends only. Now I intend to do it regularly and for people far removed from my circle. I feel like a baby learning how to walk with the goal of eventually being able to run. I do not compare my progress to established coaches. I have my own path.

We all must start somewhere. It is most important to decide to take the leap and then actually do it. Yes, there will be growing pains but indeed, pain may be needed to gain. Regrets are harder to contend with. I, for one, do not intend to have what ifs and could have beens. That is why I am taking my leap of faith.

In the end all we can truly do is give our best. Armed with sincere and kind intentions, we plant seeds, water them and cultivate as needed. Then we allow things to fall into its proper place. We adjust when necessary and ideally remain vigilant and alert for any effects outside forces may bring. Still, we can never be a hundred percent in control, and this is something we accept. Yes, we go for it and choose to be unstoppable women entrepreneurs.

Alyson MacLeod

Founder & CEO Soul Expression Sessions

https://www.linkedin.com/in/alyson-m-macleod-25111a9

https://www.instagram.com/alyson_macleod

https://www.facebook.com/alyson.macleod1

https://www.facebook.com/groups/975044462903717

http://www.soulexpressionsessions.com

Alyson MacLeod, CHC is an international best-selling author, speaker, serial entrepreneur and certified Transformational Results Coach. She is a Health, Life and Business Coach with a degree in Community, Economics and Social Development. Alyson coaches Executive and high achieving Entrepreneurial Women who have lost their drive to succeed. She teaches Executive and high achieving women strategies to find happiness, passion and confidence again to Live the Life of their Dreams by refocusing, gaining clarity and learning to live in their full Soul Expression as God intended. Her inspirational podcast, magazine and tv show called "Soul Expression Sessions" are hosted on the Wealthy Women Entrepreneurs Network. Discover more at www.wealthywomenentrepreneursnetwork.com

The Conquering Goddess:
Balancing the Warrior and the Wizard

by Alyson MacLeod

In business like in life there is always a balancing act. The Warrior business person is confident, strong and resilient. They have an attitude of Grow or Die, always are Fueled and always honours the Truth at ALL times. A Warrior sees a **Vision** → and becomes 100% **Committed** → and then strategizes on the **Action** needed to be taken to → achieve the **Results** they want. A Warrior is always in control and never worries about what anyone else thinks. They do not seek others' approval. They do not allow negativity or opinions to take over their mind. Warriors are strong, strategic and cunning. A Warrior decommits to that which does not serve them and commits to a better life in health, wealth and success 100% of the time. Their body is a temple, their money works for them and the success they have comes at a price. The Warrior does not waiver in their commitments and focus. A Warrior plays full on and Action is what moves them forward. A Warrior will act in spite of fear and feel courageous.

The Wizard embodies awareness. Everything they do or don't do is a choice, complete accountability. The Wizard creates their own story and understands that a life is determined by the focus and attention you give it. Wizards live in their higher self where they are loving, forgiving, open, compassionate, generous, caring, inclusive, accepting, intuitive and sensual. They are about Inner peace and the gift of attraction. The Wizard is calm, peaceful and centered. They meditate and use breath work to refocus and stay in their higher self. Wizard's believe life is a gift → A Present that wants us living *in the moment*. The Wizard has removed "should" from their vocabulary. They believe what is... is. Acceptance is what happens in the moment, everything else is your programming about another time and place. The Wizard knows that nothing has meaning but the meaning we give it and how we react tells the story we have around its meaning. There is no drama with the Wizard and they do not attach themselves to outcomes or things. A Wizard believes everything and everyone is connected.

The Warrior is how you live in the present. The Wizard is how you live in the moment. It is always a balance of masculine and feminine energies but once you master what that is for you, your success magnifies and becomes attracted to you like a magnet. It is that magical element that you possess that no one else does. This is the Juice behind who you are and what you stand for that propels your life forward. Whether by action or attraction, or a little bit of both, there is always time and space for You to be YOU! But balancing the Warrior and the Wizard is not an easy task.

I had become a conquering Goddess and surrendered to what God's destiny was for me. It took me an entire year with the help of a coach and Reiki master! It was a self-discovery journey that I just loved but it was scary, sad and exciting at times but eventually it was enlightening to recognize and focus on who I truly am in this world. It was in those times of unknowing in the deepest valleys, where the biggest breakthroughs happened. It was magical!! My favourite new scripture is *I Can Do All things through Christ who strengthens me.*

Do you need a vision for their life? Are you accepting what is being thrown at you? Are you in control? Or are the choices not yours? This is a sad and lonely path.

With a vision, *"a guiding star"*, you see your journey unfolding. You never need others' approval. You are an individual of integrity living in your authentic power. You are true to yourself in body, mind and spirit. When your path becomes illuminated, you can finally see what was right in front of you. Remember all growth comes from a connection with someone, so relationships are to be cultivated and nurtured. When you have mastered balance between your Warrior and Wizard, the masculine energy and the feminine energies of this world begin to work in your favour 100% of the time!

I know this is a daunting task but start with doing these three things and your life will start to look very different in just 21 days! I want you to get a cue card and write on it *"I am so grateful and thankful now that ... _____"* and fill in the blank. Mine says, *"I am so grateful and thankful now that my business revenue will surpass 6 figures by February 14th, 2022 at midnight. So blessed!"* Make sure it is relevant to you! Say it morning and night for 21 days with excitement and feeling behind it. You will attract it to you even faster.

The second is to do some deep breathing exercises every morning. Deep breathe in for 5 seconds, hold for 5 seconds and out for 5 seconds. When you get really good at this you will do it 5 times a day!

Thirdly, turn off all phones, computers and TV's at least 1 hour before bed. Allow your brain and your surroundings to also get back into balance. Read, pray, meditate, make love or take a bath. You have earned it!!

The attraction factor within the power of Intention is huge. Success likes speed. So, if you are serious about achieving entrepreneurial success then get ready for something quite magical to happen when you align your focus, feelings, action and results with your soul's purpose. You just might get what you want!! and that my lovely lady is exactly what we are here to help you do.

Book your **FREE** Soul Chat @ *yourfreesoulsession.com* and discover your Warrior/Wizard Archetype today!!

"May You Discover PURE LOVE inside the Sanctuary of your Precious Heart!" - Alyson MacLeod

Blessings!

XOXO

Roxana Valeton

CEO

First Person Care Clinic

http://linkedin.com/in/roxana-valeton-01a71456

https://www.instagram.com/rox_valeton/?hl=en

https://www.facebook.com/Roxy2011leo

https://valetonbc.com

https://Firstpersoncc.org

Roxana Valeton is a healthcare executive with a proven track record, and a success in healthcare business development, grant writing, and investment advisory. She has held diverse senior level positions from start-up to sustainability since she was twenty-five years old, in nonprofit and privately held corporations.

As a mother of two, wife, an Immigrant of Cuban origin, healthcare entrepreneur, and the oldest of two, all of this has fundamentally shaped who she is, and what her priorities are. It has fueled her commitment to create opportunities for communities from disadvantaged backgrounds, especially for women and children.

Presently, she is the CEO of First Person Care Clinic, a Federally Qualified Health Center in Las Vegas, Nevada, that provides medical services regardless of the individual's ability to pay. Mrs. Valeton is an anti-human trafficking activist and a fierce advocate of women rights, and mental health illnesses.

"It is a privilege to take part in this book, surrounded by real women that struggle everyday like me, with a self-constructive attitude. Women with a purpose that don't look back but live the present to the fullest," – Roxana

A ZunZún Within

by Roxana Valeton

Years ago, a tiny eight-month term girl was born on an Island. While she was growing up, many ailments hindered her quality of life and she could sense her parents worry about her health and her future, but her desire of taking control of her existence kindled the flames of what became her journey. That little girl is me, and she still resides within me, however, in a form of a Zunzún. She reminds me where I came from, and every time I feel like quitting, the Zunzún lights the fires of enthusiasm and reminds me of my dreams.

I migrated to the United States at the age of 21 with nothing in my pocket, accompanied by my dad and my 4-year-old son. Imagine yourself in a new country with no money, very poor english, and no friends. I began my ride with just my brains, instincts, and an innate ambition to succeed. From day one, I fought against female stereotypes and worked my way into a male-dominated corporate world. I did it all with an unyielding determination which would define a career that hasn't come to an end. I have been told many displeasing things in public, and many people have tried to make me feel futile and impractical, yet I never waver. Instead, I positioned myself next to "the untouchables," they might underestimate you until it is too late. I continue partnering with the experienced ones to learn from their successes, and I help the less fortunate to plant a small seed of hope every time I can, throughout my passage in this life. "What has hurt me in the past has become a brick in my fortress. I am proud to allow no one to fluster my credence; and that's how I want you to feel about yourself from this moment on." If you believe you don't know where you are going, it is time to re-focus and act.

My parent's guiding principles during my education were the key to helping build my personality. You can have a better life just by changing your attitude and your routine. Always remember, "Self-assurance is the full expression of your individuation." I still remember my very first job as a housekeeper in Miami Beach, making six dollars an hour. I was so grateful that I could help my dad pay for our expenses. I had a second job on the weekends, and I was learning English at night. Never complained, or compared myself to anyone. Four years later, I co-founded my first company the same day of my 25th birthday. I didn't make any money for almost a year while working every day from 8 am to almost 8 pm, including Saturdays. Towards the end, I felt I was failing but I moved away from my comfort zone and I kept holding my dreams. Presumably, it would be easy but it wasn't, and I promise you, it won't be easy for you either, but do not stress yourself. The higher you fly, the more that small problems will be replaced by bigger ones. Here are a few tips of what has helped me.

Taking care of your health is the most important part of this journey. Learning about nutrition is the first thing I recommend you to do. What you eat will decide how you feel, how you react, and how you think. I wouldn't be able to make it this far without having self-awareness to be able to figure out whether the path forward is the right one to take. Learning about how dopamine levels affect your mood, your memory and focus. The importance of your gut health is pivotal. Knowing the benefits of organic meals, and what type of diet suits you. Discover how most of the information we are told are only excuses, myths or marketing strategies for you to consume a specific product. Some foods will make you feel tired, angry, depressed or even anxious. If you constantly feel this way; eventually, you won't be able to work as a rational person, and no one will follow someone who has a house of cards just waiting to collapse. In order to become an unstoppable woman, a wealthy person, or simply be able to raise and support your kids and family, having strong balanced mental and physical health are key. Finding motivation will help you with this. I wanted to be ready for my parents when they needed me most, and make a difference in the lives of others. Never forget, you'll need a team behind you and you need more than just you to become successful. Learn how to listen to accomplished entrepreneur's advice. What you don't know is what might be keeping you stocked.

Back in Cuba, most women were working in a factory, teaching, or doing domestic work. Very rarely you'd find us in leading positions. While living there, my generation grew up without cell phones, internet or fancy electronics. I remember every struggle and how hard my parents worked day and night to try to put a meal on the table. Everything is changing, we have shown the world that instead of giving up, women are accomplishing what very few did back then.

Instead of trying to imitate others, find your own way. Be unstoppable, be unique, be fierce like a Zunzún. If you need to start over, you won't be starting from the scratch, you will be starting from the mistakes learned, from your determination, and your courage.

Be honest to yourself and everyone around you. Find your passion and you will develop a pride within you that will never let you abandon your dreams. Your story will be the one of your dreams if you nurture your knowledge. I wish you a bright future. I will be here for you if you need guidance. You truly deserve a chance of success.

Jennifer Cairns

Founder & Lead Rebel at Lady Rebel Club®, Micro-Brandologist and creator of my proprietary Rebel Brand Method™ and B.A.D. Framework™

https://www.linkedin.com/mwlite/in/jennifer-cairns

https://www.instagram.com/lady.rebel.club

https://www.facebook.com/LadyRebelClub

www.ladyrebelclub.com

https://www.facebook.com/groups/theladyrebelclub

Hey, I'm Jennifer and live in Northern Ireland with my husband, two boys and dog. I'm a neurodiverse award-winning entrepreneur, International Bestselling Author, speaker and changemaker. I'm the founder at Lady Rebel Club® where my mission is to help women entrepreneurs who are neurodiverse and/or who have a hidden disability/disorder create a business that fits their life, needs and definition of success. We do this by offering a free Facebook® community, workshops, summits, and a membership that helps you grow a successful brand that skyrockets your confidence, impact, and revenue without having to be perfect or fake. My big vision is for each of us to see that we're a goldmine with value to give and that nobody sets our limits but us. Simultaneously, to stir things up on social, business and institutional levels so we evolve hearts, minds and attitudes while creating a diverse, purposeful and even playing field that values unique experiences, thinking, talents, ideas and people.

Lady Rebel Club: Start of a Revolution

by Jennifer Cairns

Rebellion can be about adapting, fighting for and building things anew. A revolution is often needed to evolve hearts, minds, and attitudes. It can be required to shift paradigms to make room for a better way. If you are a woman*, we often find ourselves still marginalised in business. A woman who is neurodivergent or who has a hidden disability/disorder is more often overlooked and misunderstood.

I've been on this road for a while. I've taken many wrong turns and fallen in a lot of potholes to get where I am now. I'm neurodiverse, and maybe like you, I think differently to many people. I have a busy, creative mind and struggle with anxiety disorders like GAD and CPTSD. I have chronic illnesses and hidden disabilities like fibromyalgia, fatigue, IBS, seizures, nerve pain, migraines, blood cancer and more.

I say this, so you know *I get it*. After navigating this road myself, here are some key turns and shortcuts to help guide you on your road to becoming a rebel leader who creates a business where you're thrilled being your unique self and that suits your life and definition of success.

First Left: Know Your Gold

I have a saying, "You are a goldmine, don't let anyone tell you differently."

I believe we all have value to give. I've always known a big chunk of my gold is my grit. It has held me together through many waves in life and business. I have other gold, too.

It's not arrogant to value yourself and your gold. Believe in its value, your value. Others will never fully value you until you fully value yourself. I wish there'd been someone standing on the side of the road when I first started my business, jumping up and down with a sign that read, "You are a goldmine! You've got value to give! BELIEVE IT!" But there wasn't. I suppose this chapter is me jumping up and down holding that sign for you.

Next Right: Flip Your Thinking

Have you ever heard people say you sell a product best by singing its benefits? We're not products, of course, yet we need to apply the same logic to how we talk about ourselves when we're talking about being included. For too long, we've been banging on the door screaming that we need to be seen, heard, and included *because* we're women*, have a disability/disorder, or are neurodivergent. This approach can cause a lot of pushback as it makes people feel like we're forcing our way in the door.

Instead, what if we knock on that door by talking about our benefits, those unique attributes we bring. People will be more likely to open the door for us themselves and welcome the gold we have to share. Know you're gold, the benefits you bring to the table, your unique perspective and your superpowers. Start the conversation leading with THOSE. You could soon find that others will quickly see, hear and want to include you without you ever having to ask. Flipping this internal switch is paramount if we're going to flip the external ones.

Third Turn: Different Not Less

Me owning these words and their power didn't happen overnight. Doing so has skyrocketed my confidence and allowed me to rock my visibility, take massive steps and feel happier being me in my business.

We often make ideal, innovative, and impactful entrepreneurs because of the hurdles we constantly have to jump and our different brains. Knowing it's ok to be yourself (and not just say it as a hashtag) is critical for success. You're the special sauce and the engine that will drive your business forward.

It's easy to feel like you don't belong and aren't like any of your business peers. Our experiences have shaped us into the unique individual I am, and you are. Don't just embrace the fact you're different. LOVE it.

Once you own your gold, start leading conversations with your benefits and embrace that you're different, not less, you can begin the journey of building a business that suits you. You can grow a business and brand that fits your life and definition of success while being happy being your unique self.

Additional points of interest on your road to rebellion:

- Fill in knowledge gaps and ask for help when needed. Asking for help isn't weak. It's an unstoppable strength.

- Carry yourself. Running a business isn't easy. External forces alone aren't enough to motivate you to do the hard work or take action. Only you can.

- Carry others. There will be others who need to be lifted along the journey, just like others have and will raise you, pay it forward.

- Make mistakes. You'll learn faster and grow quicker if the fear of making a mistake does not freeze you.

- Remember, any opinions of your business or brand may be difficult to hear but have nothing to do with your value as a human.

- Take time to look for and appreciate the uniqueness and gold in others. #Priceless

- There is always a way to stand out with your marketing, messaging, positioning and branding. Look for the gaps in what they aren't saying or doing.

- Perfection is a myth. #Fact

- Collaboration can lighten the work, increase the impact and be good fun.

- Work hard and smart.

- Find what WAY of working is best for you. More breaks, shorter days, batching are some of the numerous ways to work IN your business, so it suits. Not every business needs to run the same way.

- Gratitude. There is always something to be thankful for. Even when things fail and the waves hitting us feel 50 feet high, focus on who/what you have and the lessons learned.

- Learn from yesterday, plan for tomorrow, yet make sure you live and enjoy today. Once spent, we never get it back.

- Lastly, remember the road to rebellion is about shaping a future where unique ideas, thinking, talents, experiences and thus people each have value. A rebel leader breathes this into their business and encourages others to do so, too. It's not enough to value your uniqueness. Appreciate others', too.

Now find, collab and connect with other rebel leaders. Lady Rebel Club® is also here for you. Together we can ensure we all arrive at the destination that sees the change in ourselves, our businesses, and the world around us we want (and need) to see.

*Any female-related terms used automatically include anyone who identifies as female or is non-binary.

Natalie Pickett

Entrepreneur, Speaker and Mentor

https://www.linkedin.com/in/natalie-pickett-74b00910

https://www.instagram.com/natalie_Pickett_Mentor/

https://www.facebook.com/nataliepickettmentor

http://www.nataliepickettmentor.com

https://www.facebook.com/groups/livingthedreamcommunity

Natalie Pickett is an award-winning business leader and much sought-after business mentor and speaker. A best-selling co-author of 'Becoming an Unstoppable Woman' Natalie has been featured in major publications including Authority Magazine, Ariana Huffington's Thrive Global and Entrepreneur.com. Natalie started her entrepreneurial career around 30 years ago, and is founder of multiple businesses, with both 6 & 7 figure success stories. Natalie generously shares insights into her triumphs and so called 'failures' – along the way, discovering that becoming unstoppable is less about hard work, and more about finding joy in your every day.

It is possible to define your own version of success and easily take the steps you need to achieve your goals. It is possible for you to not just 'Dream the Dream' but 'Live the Dream'! Passionate about sharing this with the world, Natalie shows you how in her courses and in her chapter in this book.

Living the Dream

by Natalie Pickett

I still remember the excitement when in my first business, the first sales came through. My clients were in different time zones, and I'd wake to find new bookings had been faxed through (this was pre-internet) overnight. There's something quite exciting about making sales in your sleep! The excitement when you receive sales never goes away.

I love business. People think that a 'business mind' is different to a 'creative mind', but when you create something where there was nothing, that's creative. Turning an idea into something bigger, such as a business that benefits everyone who buys from you, is undeniably creative. I love being able to do that and help others do the same.

As a serial entrepreneur, I have founded multiple businesses over the past 30 years, and I have had my share of triumphs and so called 'failures'. Along the way, I've discovered that becoming unstoppable is less about hard work, and more about finding joy in your every day. As a business mentor and speaker for more than 12 years, I share this knowledge with others, and help them to take their business and daily life from surviving to thriving.

Travel is a big part of my life and my career. After learning the ropes in Europe, I returned to Australia at age 28, and established my first business. My first business was an inbound travel company bringing visitors from around the world to see Australia. While we grew to multiple 7 figure sales, the tourism industry is subject to many external factors. You can be hit with something overnight, such as natural disasters, pandemics and acts of terrorism. Suddenly, people stop travelling and your cash flow vanishes. Even though I had managed my business through many of these disruptions, the 2007–2008 Global Financial Crisis was devastating.

As much as this 'crash' was a crisis, it was also the opportunity to create the life I really wanted. I had let my business take over from my needs. I am thankful for the lessons learned and I use that experience in my own businesses, and when helping clients create resilient businesses that support their needs and desires.

To be successful you need grit, passion and faith in the value of what you are doing. People think that going into business will give them freedom to do whatever they want, but if you're not careful, the business can take over your life. There is always a lot of test and measure, and not everything turns to gold straight away. Consistent and persistent action to keep going, even when things haven't gone as planned is needed. Being persistent is different from just working hard. Take time to get clear, get in alignment and follow the path. When things don't go as planned, you need to be agile and open to change to suit the current operating environment. Celebrate the highs and enjoy the journey. That is the sweet spot, even more than the end goal. In all my businesses I align to follow the joy. When you enjoy what you do every day, and are bringing value to others, that is when you are living the dream!

If you're just starting out in business, remember that things that seem daunting and all-consuming become second nature as you and your business evolves.

My top 10 tips on creating a business that works for you:

1. **Good support** - Being the boss can be lonely! Support can include systems and structures, but is also about learning how to support yourself. You need a good team of mentors and advisors, and learn to ask for help when you need it.

2. **Establish good foundations before you grow** - When you're starting small, create systems, templates, seek good advice on structure and then automate what you can. A strong business needs a good foundation to scale.

3. **Prioritize yourself** - If you don't prioritize what is important to you, you will become a slave to the business and others.

4. **Emotional intelligence** - Being able to observe your emotions and understand why you might be experiencing them and using them to guide you to what you need to do next. Knowing how to support your own emotional needs is one of the keys to a happy life.

5. **Empathy** - Being able to consider someone else's perspective, how they are feeling and why they may be acting a certain way.

Understanding this will be a great tool for resolving issues and when negotiating.

6. **Manage your energy** - Knowing how to read your own energy is crucial. Failure to do so will lead to burn out. If you are experiencing resistance, reset and restore your energy until you can move forward from a place of inspiration. In difficult times, take one day, or sometimes one intense hour, at a time. Then rest, re-evaluate and focus on the next task.

7. **Know your value** - Define and align to your value set and operate with integrity from there. I use my core values to guide me in life and my businesses. Operating from a place of value eliminates self-doubt and aligns with your sense of purpose. In challenging times, your values will be the driver that will get you through any negativity.

8. **Get clear on your 'Why'** - Get clear on why you are doing it, what you want to get out of it, and how much time you want to spend working on it.

9. **Define your definition of success** - Don't be influenced by what other people think that you should be doing. There's no need to do it all at once. It's okay to stay small and grow when you're ready.

10. **Don't put off living your dream life** - Are you waiting for something to happen in the future to start enjoying your success? It really is about enjoying each of the steps along the way. When

the business becomes stressful, remind yourself that business and life are supposed to be fun. Our businesses should work for us, not the other way around.

Are you ready to take your business to the next level and start living your dream life now? If this resonates with you, follow the links in my bio to access content, courses and mentoring opportunities.

Valerie Carrillo

Realtor

www.instagram.com/livinglasvegasig

https://www.facebook.com/NormaValeriaCarrillo

https://valerie.sherisesstudios.com

Living my dream as an entrepreneur. I am a mother to 3 great young adults. A wife to an extremely supportive and hardworking husband. My passion is empowering women by educating them on the home buying process and assuring them they can live a life without limits. Home ownership is the ultimate step in being independent and my goal is to educate young women in starting their real estate portfolio. I host fun events for my clients and answer any questions they may have to move them from client to buyer. I've created "The Woman's Guide to Owning Her Dream Home," which demonstrates the step-by-step process that takes the guesswork out of how to get started. I believe a female entrepreneur is strength & bravery. You have stepped out of your comfort zone and realized your worth. You believe in yourself and ignite the fire in your soul.

Love, Truth and Being a Female Entrepreneur

by Valerie Carrillo

Manifest Destiny, words that have stuck with me for decades. I believe you have to set yourself up for success. Vision boards, affirmations, meditation, making a gratitude list every morning or prayer whichever works best for you. Definitely implement one or all and stick to it. For me my week starts on Sunday. Sunday evenings I go through my emails and networking events on social media. I make sure to write down 1 or 2 of them into my planner. Writing them down on paper works best for me. I schedule anything I want to do for the week. Also anything and everything you need for your mental health. Your mental health is very important and should come first for everything else in your life to go well. Every Q4 I work on a new vision board for the following year. It's my favorite thing to do. I make it fun and invite my girlfriends over. Every morning before anything else, I thank my Lord and Savior for another day. I sit in peace and talk to Him for a bit. Once a day in my bathroom I look in the mirror and repeat my affirmations. When I'm ready for work and go to open my planner I write down what I'm grateful for that day. Before bed I make sure to thank God again for the day I had.

Love, love what you do. It's the only way to survive a long successful career. It has been my passion and pleasure to help and educate my buyers on the process of home buying. One of my greatest satisfactions has been handing over the keys to new homeowners.

Their excitement and gratitude is an amazing feeling for me. Buyers start off as buyers and have become lifelong friends. I make sure to hold their hand and walk them through the entire process making sure I explain and they understand every little part of it.

Be the truest version of yourself. Be the best you, you can be. Take care of yourself. There is only one you. Choose you. Choosing yourself is one of the most important decisions you can make. I am true and honest with my family, friends and clients. My relationship with my clients has blessed me with referral after referral. Integrity and honesty are some of the most appreciative qualities in human beings.

Freedom, I chose my career for the freedom it gives me. Being an entrepreneur has given me the opportunity to make my own schedule. I was able to take my kids to school and pick them up, go to their school functions and take them to their sports practices and games. Quality time with my kids has been amazing throughout the 2 decades of my career. If one of my kids got sick at school, I didn't have to ask anyone for time off to pick them up. I could just go and be there for them.

Being a female entrepreneur has had its highs and its challenges. No one is pushing you, you need to push yourself. It takes discipline and hard work. The business does not come to you. You need to go out and get it. Every day is a hustle. Every day you need to be prepared. Never quit learning. This is why I have a planner and write everything down.

You need to be organized so that nothing falls through the cracks. I've had great productive days filled with celebrations. I've also had some terrible days in what used to be a male dominant field. Days filled with men in my field talking down to me, reminding me how long they have been in the business. Them not realizing I've been in the business longer than them. I've had days of sexual harassment from men working in the same office. I've had to be strong and It wasn't easy. It's not a happy time when you are going through your day, especially if you have had a tough day and these men are vulgar and rude. I have also been blessed with a few men in my life that have lifted me. Male figures that have supported and pushed me. Males that have treated me like an equal and to those men I will forever be grateful. Surround yourselves with those types of peers. Male and female. Throughout the years I've had more and more female friends on the same level. Female friends that want to see you succeed. Female friends that support you and are always offering their kind words. Your circle is very important. Get rid of the negative ones in your life whether they are family or disguise themselves as friends. If they are negative and don't believe in you, you don't need them.

I know firsthand you can have your tough days in which you don't want to get out of bed. You have to push through. For years I was tired, my bones ached. I thought I was just tired from waking up early for 20 years raising kids. I rested and rested. Still I was tired. I was exhausted. I finally went to see my doctor and I found out I had an autoimmune. Now that I knew that it wasn't me it was my body things changed for me. I started watching what I ate and started meal prepping. I started taking vitamins and supplements. I started listening to my body. I know if I don't have breakfast, I'll get dizzy throughout the day. Take care of yourself. Get to know your body. I have breakfast and have a meal prepared for lunch daily. Have healthy snacks around you, you'll thank yourself later. I am here to tell you that you can push through it. This is where your "why" comes in. Who is your why? Why do you get up and do what you do? For me, my "why" is my kids and my husband. They are why I get up and push through every day. I think about creating a better life for my kids and helping my husband reach our goals. Believe in yourself and you too can be an Unstoppable Female Entrepreneur.

Lisa Shepherd

Co-Founder and Director at Bloom Bakers Ltd.
https://www.linkedin.com/in/lisa-shepherd-09bb2b20
https://www.instagram.com/bloombakers
https://www.facebook.com/bloombakers
https://www.bloombakers.co.uk
https://www.bloombakers.co.uk/about-us

Lisa Shepherd was born and raised in Germany. She has a degree in Transcultural Communication from the University of Vienna, Austria. Volunteering in the Galapagos Islands she met her British husband. They travelled the world together before settling in Leeds, UK. She has two wonderful children who are not only her pride and joy, but also her greatest teachers. Together with her friend Saskia Roskam, she founded Bloom Bakers, an online business that specialises in personalised and branded biscuits. The real product however is kindness. Not only do they help spread kindness in biscuit form, they capitalise on kindness in all aspects of the business - from the way they interact with customers and staff to the impact they have on our planet. Their vision is to introduce more female qualities to the business world, remove the stigma associated with working mothers, and run a purposeful business that enables women to combine a career with motherhood - without the guilt.

How to Bloom in business and life

by Lisa Shepherd

My entrepreneurial journey is one of nearly losing myself – but in experiencing losing myself, I found myself.

One night, about 15 months into running my business, I was lying next to my husband and told him that I was empty inside. I had depleted myself entirely. Being a new mum and setting up a business next to my part-time job, with no family support nearby, had taken it out of me.

When my friend Saskia and I decided to set up Bloom Bakers from our kitchen tables, my daughter was eight months old. Within three months, we had launched the business. In those three months we had come up with a name and logo. We had created and populated a website and social media channels, researched recipes and packaging, baked and taste tested. We had done marketing, food photography, gained hygiene certificates, registered our kitchen and got all the necessary insurances, to name just a few jobs! We didn't take on any loans, or receive any investment or outside funding. To start the business, we each put in £500; the rest was pure dedication and hard work.

Since we both have a background in digital marketing, we knew how to grow a brand online. We worked with bloggers and influencers, we approached the media with our story, we identified our USP, and optimised our webpages for certain keywords so that we could start ranking high on Google.

All of this contributed to us becoming one of the top four brands in our industry. We were mothers and marketers by day, bakers and business women by night.

Behind the scenes however, things weren't so rosy. The first two years of running Bloom Bakers nearly broke me. The morning after taking the first anti-depressant pill of my life however, I looked into the mirror, and it was as if a grey veil had been lifted. As if I could see myself again. See my life again. I was filled with a deep sense of gratitude. For what I had in my life, for how far I had come. Just like a healed broken bone, I would come out stronger.

Six months later, as I found out I was carrying our baby boy, I discontinued taking anti-depressants. My way out of that dark hole was to learn to appreciate myself, to look after myself, to rid myself of guilt and pressure.

Being a mother is all consuming. So is running a business. I did both at the same time, without learning one vital lesson first: That I cannot pour from an empty cup. All around me I see women who ignore their needs, push themselves, try to prove themselves beyond the pain threshold. Whether that is trying to portray living their best life on Instagram, or not asking their partner for the support they deserve. Women are so strong, but the flip-side is that we put up with a lot, and on many levels, to the extent that it can make us ill.

The pandemic forced me to let things go. To do things from a place of love. For others, but also for myself. I learned that self-care isn't selfish.

Elisabeth Kübler-Ross says all human emotions stem from two core emotions: love or fear. For far too long I had been running on autopilot, a busy fool, trying to do it all, driven by a fear of failure and rejection.

It was only when I started embracing my limits and boundaries, and when I started to work on myself, that my business really started to flourish.

When the first lockdown was imposed, we sent out hundreds of free "Kindness Biscuits" with encouraging messages from one person to another. During a time when we were told to separate, I felt closer to my fellow humans than ever before.

Spreading kindness and hope in biscuit form was our business' small contribution to lifting the spirits. Little did we know it would lead to a 400% increase of our B2C sales. With offices being shut and corporate events cancelled, B2B, our main revenue stream, dried up completely. Those B2C sales carried us through. We quintupled our profits that year.

During the second lockdown, I started working with Will Polston, a business coach who helped me identify my values, and what I needed to change to create a more balanced life. For the first time in my life, I set clear goals. Within three months of working with him, I quit my job in digital marketing to focus on my business. We moved the business out of our homes and into our first commercial kitchen. We employed three members of staff; all of them women, all of them mothers. We find a deep sense of purpose in creating a sustainable life for them and ourselves. One that allows us to prioritise our children, something we missed when we were employees.

Performance coach and author Jamil Qureshi says: "The price for success is paid in advance and in full". I now understand what he means. I also understand the power of being an entrepreneur.

It's not about money. Success doesn't have to be about financial gain. Living a fulfilled life in line with my values, having a healthy family, strong friendships, enjoying what I do, being well in myself, that is what success is for me. Once I turned things around, when I started prioritising my own needs, and appreciated myself and my journey, everything else fell into place.

Running a business gives you a voice. As a mother, you can make all the difference to your children's lives, but as an entrepreneur, the circle of people you can touch and inspire is much wider.

That is precisely why it is so important that you act from a place of love. That especially us women stop imitating male behaviour, no longer comparing ourselves to them, or competing with one another.

Four years on from my darkest moments, I realise I have learned more about myself in that time than in the previous 30 years. I might have come to the same conclusions eventually, but running a business accelerated it. Becoming a "mumpreneur" for me was the ultimate personal development exercise.

What makes me unstoppable is that I now know my needs, and I value myself enough to have those needs met.

I invite you to give yourself permission to Bloom too, and your business success will follow.

Danielle Archer

DocD.LMHC

Counseling, Coaching, Consulting and Advocacy.

The Artist Minds

CEO and Director of Artist Support.

Cancer Makes Me Mental Blogger.

www.linkedin.com/in/docdlmhc

www.instagram.com/docdtherapy

www.twitter.com/doclmhc

www.facebook.com/docdlmhc

Dr. Archer is a wife, mother, and entrepreneur. She is city girl at heart, born and raised in New York, and currently residing in sunny Central Florida. Danielle owns and operates DocD. LMHC, which provides counseling to cancer patients/survivors, as well as coaching, consulting, and advocacy services for a variety of mental health topics. She runs The Artist Minds, a non-for-profit which provides mental health and wellness services to music industry professionals.

Dr. Archer also maintains the blog site Cancer Makes Me Mental which focuses on the personal perspective and professional information regarding the mental health side of cancer. And she proudly sits on the Board of Directors for Thrive Clermont and Beyond the Booth. Danielle approaches her work from a combined perspective of clinical experience, life experiences and lessons that she has learned from her clients. She delights in the challenges and rewards of entrepreneurship as well as helping others.

Get Out of Your Own Way

by Danielle Archer

In 2004, I found myself living as a single mom with a 3-year-old daughter. I had relocated to Central Florida and was starting my life all over again. While I did have family down here, I had to find a job, daycare, etc. to be able to support myself and my daughter.

I was working in the mortgage industry and had taken a job with a small local broker shop. One day, my daughter got sick, and I was called to the daycare to pick her up. She had a fever and was breaking out in some sort of rash on her face. It turns out she had hand, foot, and mouth disease and was unable to go back to the daycare for several days. I contacted my boss to let him know and his fiancé (who was quasi managing his office) called me back. I remember the conversation as if it happened yesterday, she said to me "I cannot have you call in sick, we need you here, I don't even have my nanny today." That comment stung me at my core. At the time, I was on WIC and received a small amount in food stamps, my daughter's biological father was not providing any financial support, and I had a vehicle that was facing repossession. I made enough money to pay for daycare, gas, some of my living expenses, and that was it. I got off the telephone with her and felt so small, defeated, and dehumanized. There were no feelings of support or understanding from mother to mother, just a woman who was inconvenienced by not having her nanny that day. I quit that job shortly thereafter.

After that experience I knew that I ultimately wanted to work for myself. I did not know what that was going to look like and when that would even happen, but I knew that I did not want anyone to have a say over my ability to be able to be there for my child. I wanted to be there for any daycare/school activities and events. I no longer wanted to feel small, insignificant, and unimportant. So, I enrolled in an online bachelor's degree program and worked on my degree at night and on the weekends. When that was done, I started on my master's degree, thanks to my husband, Danny, and my (step)daughter, Ashley, who were able to help me out at home. I even remember working on one of my papers the night before Danny and I got married. It took me four years from completing my master's degree to become a fully licensed mental health therapist, when it took most people two years. I then enrolled in an online Doctorate degree program, which took me five years to finish. During that time, we had two more children, bought a fixer-upper house, and faced various other challenges in our lives.

I started a counseling practice in 2009. I had zero idea of what I was doing. We never learned the business end of running a counseling practice in graduate school. I was learning by doing and from different mentors that I was fortunate enough to be aligned with over the years. My business has taken many forms over the years. I questioned each change that I have made, thinking that I had to have other peoples' approval and validation that they thought it was good before I put it out in the world. Deep down I knew what I wanted to do and how I wanted to do it. I was afraid to trust myself and my instincts. I was standing in my own way. After years of doing this, I had to draw a line in the sand and say no more. I had to stop making excuses.

I worked a full-time job, shuffled kids back and forth to school, appointments and extracurriculars and went to college. I very rarely took any time off, even when I was sick, I still worked as much as I could. I was fortunate enough that if my kids were sick, they came to work with me. I sacrificed sleep, time for myself, time with my friends and family and in some cases, my sanity. However, I went out there and made contacts and connections. I got out of my comfort zone and started writing and speaking at events and volunteering my services. I learned how to build websites and how to navigate social media. I paid for advertising in different places and publications when I had the funds. I changed my company name, brand, and area of focus, and then I did it again, and then again.

There were many times when I wanted to give up, or when I felt like an imposter, or when I felt like I had no value and was never going to be a success. In the end, what I have learned is to be true to myself. To focus on what I am passionate about and what feels right to me. That collaboration is way better than competition. That my downtime for rest and self-care is just as important as burning the midnight oil. I learned to get out of my own way.

For the woman who I allowed to make me feel small, defeated, and dehumanized, my long-standing "f**k you" over the years has turned to "thank you". You were essentially my catalyst for change and for relentlessly pursuing entrepreneurship.

For the teenage girl with a dream career, for the recent college graduate full of ideas, for the single mother who has to make the choice between sending a sick child to daycare (and keeping her fingers cross the child makes it through the day) or calling out of work and potentially jeopardizing her job, for the married woman who has spent years caring for her family and now wants to do something for herself, I see you. I have been you.

If you are reading this and feel stuck, if your interests feel unattainable, if you feel unsupported, shoot me an email (docdlmhc@gmail.com) so that we can brainstorm together and perhaps give you that little push and encouragement you need to get out of your own way and on your way to bringing your dream to life.

Entrepreneurship Tips

1. It is a marathon, not a sprint.
2. Find a mentor or a few trusted, knowledgeable colleagues in your field that you can bounce ideas off of and also have a community with. Being in business for yourself does not mean you have to be by yourself.
3. Don't be afraid to put yourself out there. A "no" is an invitation for you to persevere, not to retreat.

4. Don't be afraid to change up your company's mission, services/products, etc. You want to make sure what you are putting out there is in alignment with who you are as a person. As we change and grow as individuals, our business does too.

5. Write down your goals, put them somewhere you can see them every day, along with any quotes, music lyrics, photographs, or anything else that helps motivate you and reminds you of what you are working so hard for.

Gayle Gunn

Organizing Strategist

www.gaylegunn.com

Gayle Gunn is an Organizing Strategist who specializes in space utilization. She offers a unique "outside-in" approach to decluttering that awakens the mind, body, spirit, & space connection.

Gayle's gift of spatial acuity, along with her personal journey, and her design experience working for Crate & Barrel, and Bassett Furniture, inspired her to launch her own business. She blended her passion for organizing, coaching, and design to create Ener-CHI Organizing. She now works with women and new home-based businesses guiding them on a journey to organizing their space, helping them set it up in a way that inspires, motivates, and empowers their success.

Today when she is not at home with her family or visiting loved ones, you will find her helping her clients discover and letting go of what no longer serves them.

To learn more about transforming your space to change your life, please visit her website: www.gaylegunn.com

I Quit... Again!

by Gayle Gunn

When I think about my entrepreneurial journey and how many times I quit, it often amazes me that I am still here working for myself. What a roller coaster ride of ups and downs, frustrations and excitement! It makes me wonder where the perseverance to keep going actually came from.

As it turns out, being an entrepreneur is not only about running your own business, it is about owning y*our own life*. Becoming unstoppable happens when you decide to take control of knowing who you are, loving who you are, nourishing who you are, and trusting what you are capable of.

I remember the day I decided to own my life! In 2006, my world was turned completely upside down after having gone through several life changes back-to-back. I had been let go from a five-year career. I was going through a divorce and moved out of the place I had called home for seven years. Plus, all the years of "baggage" I had carried with me. I was about to turn 30 and *my life was a total mess*!

Aside from now needing to figure out who I was, I knew I really needed to get a job. A few months into working with a colleague that I had become close with, I asked her if I came across as the trainwreck I thought I was. She looked me straight in the face and said "No. You actually carry yourself with confidence and poise". She went on to add, "The only reason I know you're a train-wreck is because you won't shut up about it!"

That was it! That was the day I decided to own my life. I was going to quit being such a train-wreck! I set out on a journey to feel on the inside the way I carried myself on the outside. Even though I had no idea what that would look like, I just knew I wanted to, and believed it was possible.

I began clearing away *all* of the clutter, letting go of what no longer served me, physically, mentally, and emotionally. I learned the power of forgiveness and what loving oneself truly meant so that I could fully love myself. I uncovered ways for knowing who I was, and more importantly who I am. A complete awakening of the mind, body, spirit, *and* space connection, thus creating my philosophy; "Organizing is a journey that isn't about having things perfectly in place. It is about being at peace with what *you choose* to keep in your life and how *you choose* to live."

It would take some time to get my life on track, and by 2008 I was living a life I loved. It wasn't until 2014, when in search of a new career adventure, and possibly leaving an industry I had been a part of for over 20 years, that I would look at my passions, skills, and life experiences. That's when it struck me…

What if I went through all those life changes not only to say *"what doesn't kill you makes you stronger"*. What if I had gone through all the ups and downs, learning to clear away the clutter from my life, in order to create something unique to offer others? What if this "Journey to Organizing Life" was meant to be someone else's survival guide!

What if I could help people organize their space and their life too? This would be my jumping off point for becoming an entrepreneur.

In the first year of running my business, I attended a conference where one of the instructors was talking about what it meant to build a business. I quickly learned what I was doing was *NOT* building a business, I was managing a glorified hobby! In learning the difference, it was as though I had quit before I even got started.

Although it would be a semi-successful hobby with over a dozen clients, which gave me the confidence to quit my career, my "business" would ultimately struggle to generate income. However, since I was now working for myself and slow with active clients, I was able to take some time off to be with my family when two of our family members became terminally ill. Meanwhile, I had run into a few additional startup road blocks and ended the year feeling like nothing was working. So, *I quit.*

I would spend a few months looking for a "real job" only to be disappointed with not finding anything fulfilling. I also kept hearing this little voice inside me saying "Don't give up! This is what you were meant to do". So, I would try again ...

The following year, while attempting to continue my "hobby", still feeling like nothing was coming together and even less was making sense, I would find out I was going to become a mom (in my 40's!). Since I didn't know what motherhood would bring, plus feeling frustrated with the lack of progress in my business and needing a solid second income, I would use these as excuses to throw in the towel. So, I quit… again!

After my 12-week maternity leave, which lasted over 24 months, I inevitably heard that little voice inside again saying "don't give up!"… I was called to give this entrepreneurial thing one more shot. Besides, I had learned so much from quitting, why give up now? I just knew this time would be different!

I quit my glorified hobby and began building my business. I quit holding on to what wasn't working and began focusing on what was working. I quit hiding behind excuses and decided to trust what I am capable of.

What I have learned about being an *entrepreneur* is that, it is not about doing all the things that run you ragged or into the ground and never quitting. It is about being grounded in who you are, and choosing between managing a hobby or running a business.

Becoming an *unstoppable woman* entrepreneur is about owning your life, giving yourself permission to let go of what no longer serves you, and *allowing yourself to quit* as many times as you need to, so that you *NEVER* give up!

Are you ready to *own your own life*? Let's talk… email me at unstoppable@gaylegunn.com

Laura Croce

Laura Croce Christian Business Coaching & Consulting

https://www.linkedin.com/company/laura-croce-christian-business-coaching

https://www.instagram.com/coachlauracroce

https://www.facebook.com/coachlauracroce

www.lauracroce.com

Laura Croce, founder of Laura Croce Christian Business Coaching & Consulting, is a successful entrepreneur who specializes in setting up profitable and well-run companies. She believes her Christian values are the reason for her success and infuses them into her business and best practices.

Laura is a certified Professional Life Coach and received her certification from Light University, an External Studies Division of the American Association of Christian Counselors Foundation.

Laura is currently a business coach in Mentor, Ohio. With her business acumen and faith, Laura helps people grow their businesses and enjoy the experience along the way.

Stay in Your Lane!

by Laura Croce

Imagine driving down the highway with great music playing. The windows are down, a warm breeze flows through your vehicle and you are truly enjoying the ride. After some miles, it comes time to take your exit. You glance at your mirrors, turn on the signal, and BAM! You hit another car even though you thought it was clear. It turns out that little Honda you just smushed was in an area hidden from your position in the driver's seat. That, my friends, is a blind spot, and they appear in more places in your life than just a commute.

As a business and life coach, I have the unique vantage point to see the bigger picture. I can see any blind spots my clients might have as they are growing their businesses. The "driver"(business owner) has a lot to look at and be aware of, just like being at the vehicle controls. There are tasks like payroll, taxes, OSHA regulations, logistics, production, employee retention, ordering, marketing, and the office needs to be cleaned on top of it all. If only one person is driving that business bus, things will start to get complicated, maybe even slip out of mind (that is, until they get run over).

I've noticed a few recurring themes with the entrepreneurs I work with. All are brilliant and successful people, but they seem to get stuck in the same speed trap of self-limiting behavior. One of the worst behaviors is taking on too much of your own business. This leads to burnout at best and business failure at worst. I hate to be the bearer of unpleasant news, but you can't do it all, friend.

Let's break it down, shall we?

"But Laura, I'm a great multitasker!" Actually, you are not. Dr. Cynthia Kubu, a neuropsychologist at the Cleveland Clinic, says we are not multitasking, rather doing individual actions in rapid succession, aka task switching. A study posted in the Psychonomic Bulletin & Review states that only 2.5% of the human population can multitask. The rest of us are mere monotaskers, meaning that our brains can only focus on one thing at a time. When we try to multitask/task switch, we lose a lot of efficiencies. Most studies on the subject all seem to conclude that you are pretty awful at multitasking. You actually save more time and sanity if you do just one thing at a time.

"But Laura, I cannot trust my employees to do some of these tasks; I have to do them!" Ahhhh, this one is a doozy of an unhelpful thought. Most often, when my clients present me with this, the issue is the employee is not trained (if at all) to do said job. Oh, the irony! If you do not make time to prepare your employees, you will not make good employees and if you did train them and they cannot perform the task, they are still your employees because...? The business cannot grow if you are the only one working on it, and redlining at that. This leads us to the following limiting thought:

"But Laura, I cannot afford help!" Then your business will not grow. Einstein put it best, "Insanity is doing the same thing over and over and expecting different results." If you are running yourself and your business into the ground, keeping only you on the payroll will not cut it. Your mindset needs to shift from the "lack" attitude and begin to think of how much more money you can make with a team behind you.

Now, I am not doling out this advice without experience. I was in those shoes for a long time. My skill set allowed me to do many things required of my business, and I was able to learn anything else that did not cover. This all kept the plates spinning in the air…for a while. I, like so many other entrepreneurs, fell into the false sense of security that is our zones of excellence.

Dr. Gay Hendricks, the author of *The Big Leap*, was a big inspiration for me to break out of this mindset. He explains that we have "zones" for our gifting; sometimes, we are naturally good at things, others not so much. The trick is not knowing what you are good at versus bad, and the trick is differentiating between what you are good at and what you have GREATNESS. For a long time in my business, I was operating in my zone of excellence rather than the ultimate zone of genius. The zone of genius is the space where I perform at my best. Dr. Hendricks explains that many people hit their zone of excellence and remain there without genuinely experiencing the extent of their gifts or potential.

Once I came to this truth, I decided to outsource anything outside my zone of genius. I am a master at networking; I can connect almost everyone and everything, but when it comes to bookkeeping and taxes, not so much. I meet regularly with a financially savvy person who keeps track of my expenditures and creates my financial reports. I delegate almost EVERYTHING, and I am proud of it! Delegating clears my plate so that I am only working on the things I love to work on and the things in which I excel. My first piece of advice to help you start delegating: figure out what you least like to do, then hire someone to do that task for you.

I also suggest getting yourself a coach or business consultant. Consider them the "Collision Avoidance System" for your business bus. Much like a new car's system will alert if you are about to smush that Honda riding your blind spot, a coach will point out these areas that are hidden just beyond your mirrors.

As you travel on the success highway, remember: stay in your lane and delegate as if your business depends on it, because it does!

Jenny Ngo

CEO & Founder of Purpose To Profits Coaching

http://linkedin.com/in/jennythaongo

https://www.instagram.com/jennyngo_official

https://www.facebook.com/groups/6figurecoachandhealer

https://www.purposetoprofitscoaching.com

https://www.purposetoprofitscoaching.com/GetMoreClients

Jenny Ngo, is an intuitive business coach and master healer. Together with her husband--Dan, they help coaches and healers to quantum leap their business to 6 Figures doing what they love with more Income, Impact and Freedom using the proven The Organic Client Attraction Blueprint.™ They specialize in helping coaches & healers to launch and fill their 1:1 and group programs with organic marketing strategies + mindset and energy healing support so they can take actions to implement the aligned strategies and get results. Jenny is a business psychic, bestselling author, suicide survivor, and a featured speaker on well-known global telesummits, such as You Wealth Revolution, From Heartache To Joy and among other coaching & healing summits. Prior to coaching, Jenny worked in the medical field as an RN & Certified Nurse-Midwife for over 12 years. They love spending time together with their 2 kiddos, traveling to the beach and fun places.

Your Business Can Be Successful!

by Jenny Ngo

One of the common questions I get asked when I do Intuitive Business readings is, "Will my business be successful?"

According to the U.S. Small Business Administration over 50% of small businesses fail in the first year and 95% fail within the first 5 years.

WOWW! Isn't that CRAZY?

This is exactly why we're on a mission to change this...

Hi, if we haven't met I'm Jenny Ngo. My husband Dan and I are intuitive business coaches & master healers. We specialize in helping coaches & healers using organic marketing strategies to start or scale their online business to 6 figures doing what they love with MORE Income, Impact & Freedom.

More Money = More Lives Changed

More Lives Changed = More Impact

We believe when more heart centered entrepreneurs make money and have thriving businesses, we can be better humanitarians and philanthropists in the world.

In this chapter, I'll share with you business strategies and the mindset you'll need to have a successful business.

Your business is an extension of who you are.

80% is Mindset. 20% Strategies

We need the energetic clearing and healing support to help us re-program and re-wire those deeply ingrained unconscious limiting beliefs and patterns that are in the way of our success. So that we can have the BEST chance of succeeding in our business.

The very thing that we want, we also at the same time unconsciously push them away through self-doubts, fears, and resistances. It's like we're launching the rocket ship of our desires, then we also launch the rocket ship of destruction, canceling them out before it gets to manifest in our life and business.

3 MUST-HAVE Ingredients For A Successful Business:

#1 Right aligned strategy

#2 Right story/belief

#3 Right emotional state

We need all 3 in order to have a thriving and fulfilling business.

In addition, here are the things you need to get clear on when it comes to having a successful business.

✅ **Connect to your Vision/Purpose.**

Your Vision/Purpose has to be bigger than your fears. Why you do what you do? It's important to align to your Soul's Purpose. People buy who you are and what you stand for.

✅ **Position yourself as an authority/expert in your field ASAP.**

Because there's a lot of noise in the market, you need to stand out from the crowd. What do you want to be known for?

✅ **Get clear on your Niche (who you help) & Message (how you help them).**

Niche & Messaging are key business foundations. It's *super* important. The quicker you own your niche and message, the more traction you'll have. Pick a chakra and take it to 100K like one of my mentors said. If new, you can "date" a niche for 3 months and see.

Common mistakes: Niche too general or keep changing niches. Then, you probably have limiting beliefs around what it means to niche down.

With messaging, talk in your ideal audience's language. Speak directly to them by using their words. Lead with TANGIBLE outcomes. Oooh, I want to hire [Your Name].

I help___(niche)___ **who**___ (problem/situation)___ **to get**___ (want/desire)___ **by** ___(your method).

When done right, you'll call out those you want to work with and at the same time repel those that are not your target clients. Marketing is easier when you're clear on your niche and messaging. It's like swimming downstream.

Common mistakes: Leading with "processes" or modalities instead of tangible outcome. Using your language instead of your ideal audience.

✅ Have an engaging audience/tribe.

Common problems I see from participants in our Free Get More Client$ Challenge, "I don't know where to find my ideal clients" or "I don't have an engaging audience." It's important to grow a bigger audience who love what you do and want what you have to offer. Otherwise, you can be the "best kept secret". Once you are clear on your niche and messaging, it's much easier to know where your ideal clients hang out. Then, position yourself in front of them.

For example, go to Facebook groups or places they hang out and start to connect and build relationships. Have an effective and authentic way to bring them to your ecosystem.

✅ Create content that converts.

Content is your marketing. Content that positions yourself as an authority and builds affinity the Like-Know-Trust factor. Most ideal clients need 7 to 12+ touchpoints and they buy from those that they trust. It's important to create engagement and give value up front.

3 Content Marketing Rules:

Entertaining

Engaging

Educational

When done right, your content marketing will do the heavy lifting during sales/enrollment conservations.

Things to keep in mind for content that converts. Clients always think about their top of the mind *problems* and top of the mind *goals/desires*. "What's in it for me?" When you talk about these things, you always get their attention. Not to mention, the average human attention span decreased to 8 seconds. That's less than a goldfish. What this means is that shorter posts and videos do better.

When creating content, keep the end in mind. "How do you want your ideal audience to think and feel?" You want to elicit emotion (state change) when consuming your content. That's how they're going to connect with you at a deeper level.

✔ Have an irresistible offer ascension model for your business.

I recommend you have an ascension model for your coaching/healing business so that your clients know what's the NEXT STEPS with you.

The offer needs to be irresistible. It's crazy for your ideal client to say "No" to; whether it's to join your Facebook group, book a call with you, or hop onto your program. Anytime, you're not getting the conversion, then you need tweaking. Is the offer irresistible enough? Or is it an audience issue?

Remember to seed your next step and handle objections through storytelling and know that social proof is the new marketing.

I trust you're getting value. If you're a coach or healer, and you're ready to launch/grow your business and looking for *hands on* support and guidance, then this is for you.

I'm looking to work with a small group of coaches & healers for Free to help them get hot organic leads and clients without paid advertising in our upcoming Get More Client$ Challenge. Reserve your spot via link in my bio.

Remember, your business can be successful. **Dream Business + Dream Life!**

Heather Stokes

Financial GPS, CEO

Partnered with, Primerica

Life/small business insurance agent, district leader,

Financial Consultant.

https://www.linkedin.com/in/heather-stokes-benton-899624204

https://www.instagram.com/heathersfinancialfocus

https://www.facebook.com/financiallyfocusedfamilies

https://www.primerica.com/heatherstokes&origin=customStandard

I am a wife, mother, homeschooler and business owner. I am a giver, a motivator, a developer and I do not except the answer no. I only see it as a challenge. My road to success has changed many times. Life has derailed my journey and I have built a new path each time. I went to college for Forensic Psychology worked for multiple government agencies over the next eight years. When I met my husband he was a flight attendant and owned a limousine business. We lived a lavish life. 9/11 was our first major setback, three years later he suffered major injury and then pancreatic cancer at 40. I could have given up, but with three girls to depending on us that was not an option. I had to learn how to be creative with money. Now it is my mission to help others to go from surviving too thriving.

Faith, Focus and Financial Growth

by Heather Stokes

As I sit down to write my chapter there is so much swirling in my mind. Where do I start, how do I explain my journey and what can I share that will be the most impactful. Many times, I look back on my life as chapters in a book. As women, we have expectations and societal roles assigned throughout our lives. Looking back, I did what was expected of me and lived up to the duty I felt assigned to. One day I woke up and realized I had lost myself, and needed to take control of my legacy.

I grew up in a middle-class family. Both my parents were the first people in their families to go to college, so college was a must in my house. I was fortunate they paid my tuition, but living expenses and fun were on me. I remember working the graveyard shift till 7 am then sleeping in the car for two hours and going to class at 9 am. Later catching a cat nap in the afternoon and back to work again. Somehow, I still found time for friends, family, and fun. I graduated with a degree in Psychology and a double minor in Criminology and Forensics. My first job was with the in-jail drug program. I learned how to listen with an open mind and a non-judgmental heart. Helping them find a new mindset to start a new life without crime, drugs, and violence. After two years, I helped start a pilot program for mental health and forensic psychology in the jail system. Helping mentally ill non-violent offenders get back on medication and in support programs. I sat on committees and in courtrooms with judges and county leaders. At times it was mind-blowing these accomplished leaders 2-3 times my senior were even listening to my recommendations on how to best serve this population of people. This time in my life taught me confidence, self-worth, and humanity.

During this time, I also met my husband. When we first met, he was a flight attendant with Delta Airlines and owned a limousine service. The idea of being a business owner was new to me. I quickly learned the benefits and challenges of being a business owner. For a while, we were on top of the world. Flying places on a whim, traveling in style. Our business was growing, our professional careers were on an upward track. 9/11 was our first major setback. He was furloughed for a year, we had to restructure because like for most of those affected the bills kept coming. Thankfully we still had the business, but people were not renting limos as much as before. We downsized and sold annual packages to survive. About a year later he was brought back full-time. When life threw us another curveball. He suffered a major injury in flight and was placed on leave. 9 surgeries later and 6 months of physical therapy he still physically could not return. After 10 years he had to say goodbye to his career with Delta. It was a crippling blow for our family. We had just taken full custody of his then 10-year-old daughter. It was again time to restructure. This time in my life taught me adaptability, survival, and determination.

I took on a new position with the sheriff's office in the child protection division. I helped families' during challenging situations, of course, there were sad days where I had to remove children for their safety. I like helping families improve their lives, but I quickly learned I was not cut out for bureaucracy and politics. When I became pregnant with my first child, I left knowing I did not want to be pregnant in this environment. It was what I experienced there that would later push me into entrepreneurship, homeschooling my children, and taught me humility.

Just when I thought I had seen and survived it all life slapped us in the face and showed me I hadn't seen anything yet. My stepdaughter was 14, my daughter was 18 months old when my husband was diagnosed with a large pancreatic mass and told he had less than 3 months to live unless he had it surgically removed and there was no guarantee. We had a few short weeks to get our affairs in order and prepare for the worst. We spent a small fortune filing legal paperwork just in case he didn't survive. We had very hard conversations I never imagined having with my husband, who was only 40 years old at the time. He survived the 6-hour surgery but physically, medically, and emotionally he changed. It was a long 8 months of recovery. It's been amazingly almost 10 years. It's been a hard road and he has had some major medical setbacks. We had to close the business, sell cars, and assets and lived off those for several years. God blessed us with another daughter. We downsized and restructured again. These hard years taught me unconditional love, faith, and perseverance.

I enjoy being a wife, a mother, homeschooler, cooking, baking and making memories every day. We have lived with the fear of losing him for so long that we were simply existing in survival mode. I had gotten lost in surviving and I forgot about thriving. I couldn't just give up, with three girls depending on me. I set out on a mission to change the direction of my life and build a legacy for my children. It was through this refocusing I found a new mindset, new goals, and the peace of mind I had missed for years. Knowing I have a plan and it is attainable. Now it is my mission to help others to go from surviving to thriving. It has been through the path I am walking now that I can understand wellness, hopefulness, and experience financial freedom.

The reality is we don't plan to fail, we fail to plan. Being prepared in business and life for the knockdowns is key to success. My advice to you is don't beat yourself up if you fail, check your ego at the door. Your life does not get better by chance, it gets better by change. The good news is you have a chance every day to make a change. As you go on your journey through entrepreneurship, know the road may be challenging, not everything will go your way and that is ok. Adaptability is what will make you unstoppable. Have faith in your mission and focus on the impact you are making. Success is attainable with faith, focus and financial growth.

Lauren Weiss

Cycle Align

MCHC & MCLC

Female Cycle Advocate

https://www.linkedin.com/in/lauren-e-weiss-female-cycle-advocate-00537a41

http://www.instagram.com/thescarletsanctuary

https://www.facebook.com/profile.php?id=100046109392085

www.cyclealign.com

www.cyclealignme.com

Lauren Weiss helps women prosper in life, business and health by leveraging and understanding the power of their monthly cycle with her exclusive Cycle Align Method™.

Lauren has a lifelong history of hormonal and menstrual cycle mayhem. She went on a quest to understand her body, her cycle and her innate feminine genius. Along with her deep research and self-awareness, she began to feel energized, creative, and productive again. Her focus then began to truthfully understand female hormones during the different cycle phases and how women can leverage them to their benefit. Lauren's research and new understanding about the TRUTH of a woman's cycle - has guided her to now be on a mission to debunk the myths, shame and false understanding of the female body and cycle. Her wish is that every woman feels connected to their internal power and hormonal cycle by tapping into their own feminine genius.

Work Like a Woman, Get Paid Like a Man

by Lauren Weiss

What if I told you that you are not utilizing one of the greatest power sources available to you at this very moment which could make you more successful both in business and life? Would you be interested to know what it is? Of course! What if I next mentioned that most people feel that this power source is a liability, an inconvenience, a curse? Still curious? This great power source is our menstrual cycle!

You read that right, one of our greatest assets as unstoppable women entrepreneurs is Aunt Flo, Crimson Tide, Shark Week, our period. Here's a secret, years ago, my menstrual cycle was my greatest pain and suffering. Let me explain.

I have personally dealt with menstrual cycle mayhem most of my life. I started my cycle when I was 16. Immediately I started having complications. Through the excruciating pain, impossible mood swings, heavy bleeding, and constant exhaustion I was diagnosed with Von Willebrand disease, Endometriosis, and PCOS. Two different doctors told me I would never be able to have a child. It was five years into my marriage that I miraculously became pregnant! However, my delivery wasn't as joyous. I nearly died while giving birth to my beautiful daughter and eventually needed to have a hysterectomy at the young age of 30.

Something had to change. I wanted to ensure what I went through would not end up being my daughters' future. I went on a quest to understand my body, my cycle, and how they connected to the world around me. Armed with my deep research, self-awareness, and new habits I began to feel energized, creative, and productive again. My focus turned to truly understanding female hormones during the different cycle phases and how women can utilize this biological resource. I am focused on helping women business leaders lean into their bodies, find harmony, and connect with their cycle to enhance their business, life, and relationships with the Cycle Align Method™.

The Cycle Align Method™ utilizes our ability to transform throughout the month. Women's infradian rhythms and cyclic nature show in the ebbs and flows of our mental, physical, and emotional changes, impacting how we perceive and perform in various circumstances. When we can work with our bodies and its hormonal fluctuations and become hyper-aware of our abilities and talents and when best to use them, we become unstoppable!

Ready to geek out with me? Let's get familiar with our cycle! The menstrual cycle consists of four phases: Menstrual, Follicular, Ovulation, and Luteal. I like to look at them as Introspective, Imaginative, Magnetic, and Enterprising.

Phase 1-Menstrual or Introspective:

You've hit a low point! All your hormones are at the lowest level they will be during the cycle. Trust me, this is a good thing. This signals the body that there isn't a fertilized egg and it's time to shed the old and start again with the new. Just like winter your body goes into hibernation.

This is a great time to be introspective and go inwards. Take the time to slow down and evaluate what's going on in your business. Use your feminine genius or intuition to see what's going well and what needs to be released. Take this pause or slower pace to plan for the upcoming month. Write a copy for those blog posts, new launches, or emails. Simply sit still with your thoughts and come up with new ideas for your business. Remember this is a time to relax, reflect and release.

Phase 2-Follicular or Imaginative:

You're on the rise! At least your estrogen is. During this time an egg develops in the ovaries and the uterine lining begins to thicken. Just like spring, the follicular phase is time for new energy and creativity.

Leverage this phase to start new projects, map out ideas, brainstorm with your besties, have those meetings you've been putting off, or start to build your network with different events. Just like spring flowers and warmer weather after a long cold winter, use this new energy and vitality to take leaps of faith in your business and watch it grow from mere buds into full bloom. Dream big girlfriend!

Phase 3-Ovulation or Magnetic

Let's get eggy with it! Estrogen is at the highest point that it will be during this cycle. An egg matures and is released ready for fertilization. Just like the sun in the summer, babe, this is your time to shine!

Seize this high-energy opportunity in your cycle to collaborate and communicate. Schedule your interviews during this time. Need a raise? This is the optimal time to have that talk with your boss or clients. Be in the spotlight and on stage with public speaking events. Record your videos for social media and courses and you'll be on the way to becoming the next big influencer! You'll feel unstoppable and be truly irresistible. Go ahead and be seen!

Phase 4-Luteal or Enterprising

It's business time! Your progesterone is at its highest point and hormone levels begin to drop. A fertilized egg will embed itself in the uterine wall. Just like summer fades into fall, our time to shine moves towards being more industrious, studious, and hyperaware. This is the most potent time of your cycle!

Take advantage of this phase to accomplish the more tedious tasks like accounting, decluttering, organizing paperwork, or other administrative tasks. Take this opportunity to schedule events, celebrate achievements, or move forward with your product or program launches. It truly is all about the details in the Luteal phase. Just like different events happen during the fall, such as gathering in anticipation for the coming winter, you too will be in a state of preparation. This is a great time to wrap up projects or other matters that are ready to finish their cycle.

When we grant ourselves the grace to show up as who we are and work like a woman, there is no other option than to be an unstoppable woman entrepreneur and get paid like a man! Begin to experience the power of leveraging your unique feminine rhythms in your business and life by emailing me at bauw@cyclealign.com today!

Melissa Porterfield

The Leadership Vibe
Founder and Chief Coaching Officer
www.linkedin.com/in/melissa-porterfield
www.instagram.com/theleadershipvibe
www.facebook.com/melissa.l.porterfield
www.theleadershipvibe.com
www.silkmountain.com

Melissa is a sought-after expert on the top three challenges that impact women entrepreneurs, intuitive coaching, and building resilience in the face of adversity. She has been featured in Empowering Women Magazine, seen on CBS News, ABC, Fox, and NBC, and has had her business displayed on the Reuters Building in Times Square (that was exciting!). She also speaks at professional events. After over 20 years in Human Resources, Melissa started her business in 2017 after an unexpected position elimination.

Today, when she's not traveling or going to see live music, you'll often find her helping women entrepreneurs overcome Imposter Syndrome, second-guessing themselves, the fear of losing everything and ending up on the street. She also teaches women how to tap into and use their intuition to make reliable business decisions, gain new insights, drive innovation, and most importantly, develop unstoppable confidence. In addition, she works with women entrepreneurs experiencing severe adversities.

Building Your Resilience

by Melissa Porterfield

We lead busy lives and frequently carry extra responsibilities that require us to build resilience. Staying in balance to move forward, whether we work for someone or have our own businesses, helps us navigate unexpected challenges and sometimes catastrophes that inevitably show up in our lives. While there is no way to guarantee that we will be free from an unexpected job loss, business decline, health issues, or loss of a loved one, we can learn resilience.

In my case, it started with getting COVID-19 two weeks after my birthday in March of 2020. I was sick for a month and didn't remember much about it. Following my illness, I struggled with Post-COVID Syndrome for a year and finally had to take a break from my business.

Following my second vaccination and after my Post-COVID symptoms disappeared, I started feeling sick again in June 2021. I pushed myself to keep going and got progressively worse through the summer until my husband called 911 late on a Sunday night. I spent a week in the hospital, finally was released on a rainy Friday afternoon, diagnosed with an illness I had never heard of, and the knowledge that it was both chronic and incurable. It required that I take steroids the rest of my life. I was happy to go home, but I was also terrified of what this new life would look like without a team of medical professionals taking care of me as I struggled to get the steroids just right.

Three days after returning home, I received a call from my largest client telling me that they had hired a full-time employee and ended my consulting arrangement. My fear increased as I contemplated how the hit to my income and my inability to work would impact my ability to start over in all areas of my life. The following week brought more bad news and ended with a terrifying car accident two weeks later. I was flat on my face, feeling incapable of finding a way out.

I was left wondering what I was going to do about any of it. Fortunately, good friends, one of my mentors, and my daughter helped clear my head and began to define a new path forward.

I realized that I needed to build resilience to get me through everything that had snowballed into one giant mess. Below are suggestions that work, and I encourage you to try all of them:

- **Take stock of what's happened.** This helped me understand that my perspective of what had happened wasn't discoloring my reality. In my case, my perception that I couldn't find a way out of the mess I was in was only perception. I journaled every day and studied my situation to clarify exactly where I was and started my action plan.

- **Chunk goals into mini goals.** My larger goals were to launch a new coaching program, increase my revenue, reduce expenses, and get my body in balance. When I looked at the magnitude, it was overwhelming. I reviewed each and broke them down into small manageable chunks, followed by scheduling time into my calendar every day to focus on each. I also scheduled breaks and lunch to ensure I stayed on track with my health.

- **Celebrate the small wins.** I captured every accomplishment during my day and took time to savor my progress. One of my mentors advised me to focus on the task at hand, take a moment to celebrate each accomplishment and try to go a little farther the next day. My daughter also helped by suggesting I capture the smallest of achievements, down to making my bed so that I could see a pattern of progress there, as well.

- **Practice optimism.** Tied closely to celebrating small wins, practicing optimism meant taking time at the end of the day to reflect and journal about what happened that day and what went right. I could see progress, and I shared my more significant wins with friends or family instead of telling everyone I was fine. Shortly after starting this practice, I found the overwhelm fading away.

- **Breathe.** One of the first physiological responses to a shock is that the breath gets shallow and rapid. The response makes it more challenging to get up, take stock, and plan for recovery. When I took breaks, or if I noticed that I wasn't focusing on the task at hand, I would stop and practice a breathing exercise I had learned in a Kundalini yoga class years ago. I found that it grounded me back into my body and refocused me.

- I started by closing my eyes and putting my hand on my belly.
- I breathed in slowly through my nose for 4 seconds and focused on filling my belly with air.
- I held that breath for four and focused on relaxing my body.
- I breathed out slowly through my mouth for a count of four, feeling the air leave my body. At this point, I felt relaxation settling in.
- I held my breath again for 4 and went back to my inhale. I do 3-5 repetitions of this box breath. It always helps.

- **Find a support team.** Knowing I had people I trusted to turn to was a lifesaver. Whether it was a friend, a mentor, health care professional, or joining a support group, I knew I had someone to reach out to when things got challenging. Building my resilience was not a one person job!

- **Work toward balancing all areas of your life.** Had I chosen to only work on my business without attending to the rest of my life, progress was not possible. I was careful to put my health first, eat properly, rest when I could, sleep through the night, take an evening walk, and practice optimism. All helped me focus on my goals.

Having committed to these practices, I found my way out. I did have what I needed to achieve my goals. I hope it does the same for you. While we can't fully control unexpected life-altering challenges, we can choose how we respond. Wishing you the best on your journey!

Olivia Radcliffe

Founder of The Bluebell Group
and Creator of The Mom Boss Society
www.linkedin.com/in/momboss-olivia-radcliffe
https://www.instagram.com/thebluebellgroup
https://www.facebook.com/thebluebellgroup
https://thebluebellgroup.com
https://www.mombosssociety.com

Boy Mom, Dog Mom, Marketing Coach, and Mom Boss Extraordinaire. Olivia Radcliffe is a much sought-after expert in all things marketing. Olivia specializes in helping mompreneurs scale their businesses to 6+ figures without sleazy sales tactics, so they can focus on what really matters most to them. She firmly believes that women don't have to choose between being a great mom/wife/partner and being a successful entrepreneur.

Olivia is also a Women Empowerment Speaker, Podcast Host, and Author. Her membership, The Mom Boss Society, has been featured as one of the top growing communities for moms in business. Spending time with family is incredibly important to Olivia, and when she's not collaborating with other amazing Mom Bosses, she can usually be found on a walk with her son and German Shepherd.

To learn more about Olivia and how she can help you grow your business, visit https://thebluebellgroup.com.

Mom Boss Rising: Live Your Dream Life

by Olivia Radcliffe

Throughout my life, there have been two Truths I've known for certain.

First, that I was going to be a mom.

Second, that I was going to be the CEO of my own company.

The first Truth was a gut instinct. A deeply rooted feeling that I could never really explain, that persisted even after multiple doctors told me that I might never be able to get pregnant.

The second Truth came from Mrs. Frech.

Mrs. Frech was my kindergarten teacher. One day after class, Mrs. Frech declared to my mom that my organizational and time management skills were off the charts and that I was going to be the CEO of my own company. This didn't shock my mom, but, by putting words to it, Mrs. Frech breathed life into a dream I hadn't even understood I had yet.

Three years later, I started my first official business. (By "official," I mean I had an invoice pad and a special pen.) It was a lawn care company. I had four customers, a lawnmower named Cindy, and a rather intense fear of snakes after I accidentally ran over one while mowing Mr. Stafford's yard.

Over the next several years, I started several more entrepreneurial ventures (including an actual commercial lawn care company, with a fleet of mowers and special sticks to gently poke the snakes away.) Eventually, I found my calling with The Bluebell Group, when I discovered that my knack for marketing could help women find their freedom through growing their own businesses.

I found myself making a real difference in the world and loved every minute of it. My clients' businesses were growing and my business was growing. Then my life changed forever.

I had my son, Greyson, on a beautiful sunny winter day. When we came home, it was bliss. (Albeit a painful, sleep-deprived, hormonal version, but bliss nonetheless.)

And then COVID-19 hit.

Within weeks, we were on lockdown. With the injuries I had sustained during delivery and Greyson's 12-day-old status, our pediatrician advised that I self-quarantine with him and not let anyone in the house. Anyone.

Suddenly, I found myself alone. A brand-new solo mom, healing, figuring out breastfeeding – figuring out *everything*, for that matter – while also keeping my household afloat and my business running.

Despite everything on my plate though, and the criticisms I faced, I wasn't willing to let my business crumble. In fact, I was more determined than ever. My "WHY" behind my business had never been clearer. I wanted to show my son that he can pursue his passions. That he can make a difference. That he, like his Mama, is unstoppable.

When it comes down to it, I believe there are three key elements to being unstoppable:

1. Clarity

To achieve any goal, you must know what it is. You must be able to visualize it, to understand what your definition of success is. Without that clarity, all you're doing is busy work. Spinning your wheels, throwing things against the wall and hoping they'll stick.

When you're clear on what your objective is, it becomes infinitely easier to cut through the clutter and make purpose driven decisions.

Ultimately, real clarity starts with you. It's the heart of what you want to accomplish through your business, for yourself, your loved ones, and those you serve. Your business can allow you to do what's important to you. When you have clarity around that purpose, that's when your passion and your purpose can truly align, and the real magic starts.

Here's the clarity test I use:

1. **Are you able to visualize your goal?**
2. **Are you able to write it down?**
3. **Can you describe your goal to others, including the WHY behind it?**

If you can do those tasks, then you've achieved clarity.

2. Confidence

Being clear on what you want is one thing, but you also need to have the confidence that you can – and will – achieve your goals, no matter what obstacles you face.

The truth is every entrepreneur is going to fail at one point or another (and usually at multiple points…). Your confidence in yourself is what determines whether those failures will stop you in your tracks or become opportunities to learn and grow beyond your original limitations.

When you have confidence in yourself and trust your intuition, YOU can be YOUR best coach and make powerful decisions that otherwise fear might have withheld.

However, it's also natural to have your confidence waver at times. Here are the steps I take when that happens to me:

1. **Create a "hype file" of your past successes and rave reviews for you to remind yourself how amazing you are.**
2. **Seek counsel from a like-minded community.**
3. **Set small goals for yourself that you can easily accomplish. Nothing helps build confidence like a series of successes.**

3. Capability

Now, it's great, to know what you want and be confident you'll get it. But that's not necessarily going to take you the distance. You also must walk the walk and take inspired action to get there.

We each have our own unique sets of strengths, weaknesses, talents, passions, experiences, and qualifications. Familiarize yourself with your strengths and lean on them to accomplish your goals.

If something doesn't fall on your list of natural capabilities, you can decide whether you'd like to develop that capability or hire someone who already has that as a strength.

Ultimately, your business is meant to enhance your passions and be a means to living your purpose. It's crucial, then, that you shape your business and everything in it – your offers, marketing strategy, and schedule – around *your* unique capabilities.

My friend, if there's one thing you get from this chapter, please let it be this:

It is possible.

You can be a great mom/wife/partner/sister/daughter/friend AND a successful entrepreneur.

You CAN have it all.

You just have to be willing to declare yourself unstoppable and go get it.

Priya Ali

Energi Living 365

www.linkedin.com/in/priya-ali-3237487

https://www.instagram.com/startliving365

https://www.facebook.com/priya.ali

www.living365wellness.love

www.energimagazine.love

Priya Ali, a dedicated entrepreneur, wife and mother of four children and four fur babies. She has led a successful personal and executive coaching practice, Energi Living 365, since 2007. After dropping out of high school at the age of 17, she quickly developed her entrepreneurial skills and never looked back. Energi Living 365, is dedicated to enabling dramatic personal and professional growth amongst its clients. Through highly personalized coaching and guidance, Energi Living 365 empowers clients to establish positive, productive thought processes and behaviours. Priya also possesses unique intuitive abilities as a third generation Intuitive, Healer and Medium, that she applies in each of her service offerings. This intuitive capacity allows her to quickly extract valuable insights from individuals and social groups, providing clients with guidance that is both objective and keenly insightful.

Priya Ali has cultivated her natural talent through a wide range of professional certifications and accreditation to maximize her capacity to support the personal, professional, spiritual and physical goals of her clients.

The Keys to Be Me

by Priya Ali

The key to your front door will not open the key to my front door. The keys to your life are exclusive to you, and your purpose is to find the doors that your keys unlock, to lead you on your individual life journey.

In 1989, I was 17 years old and was faced with the fact that my parents and I had very different ideas as to how my life should unfold and who should be making the decisions. Their lack of support and confidence in my ability to lead my life, led me to drop out of high school and leave home. I had my first part time job as a library page when I turned 12 and spent the subsequent years simultaneously working multiple part time jobs while attending school. They ranged from a real estate secretary, to a retail clerk, to a photography assistant to data entry. With my self declared wealth of experience, I assumed it would be easy for me to find employment and I did. I was hired as a file clerk for a leasing company, paying me 17K annually with full benefits. It also came with the perks of outings to baseball games, golf and restaurants where I was able to enjoy cocktails as nobody seemed to realize I was below the legal drinking age. After about 6 months there, I mended fences with my parents and they tried to convince me that I should return to high school. Not fully sold on their argument, I returned to night school and worked towards my diploma, while keeping my full time job.

While I loved having the money, I realized that there were limits to where I could grow and go in that company with the skill set and qualifications I had. After shocking my boss that I was only 18, I resigned and returned to a new high school to complete the final year. With no interest or the necessary credits to attend university, I applied to several community colleges. I was absolutely thrilled to receive acceptances into multiple schools for radio and television broadcasting. Once again, my parents had a different mindset, and directed me towards the local community college where I was able to receive free tuition since my father was employed there. General Business with the accounting track is the program they stuck me in. While I was identified as gifted at the age of 6 in elementary school and always had a great head for numbers, my heart certainly didn't beat for accounting. Once again, the differences of opinion between my parents and I, contributed to me leaving that program and eventually leaving home.

I managed to land a job as a nanny. As someone who was always drawn to children I felt I had a calling to work with them. I began part-time studies on my own dime at night and completed my diploma in Early Childhood Education. While the program taught us about children, I really felt as though it gave me the greatest insider information on the inner workings of each adult I knew. What I would later come to realize is that the freedom that children embody is what drew me to them. The freedom to just be themselves at any time, in any and every way.

Due to government cutbacks I didn't land a job in my field, but I did meet my first husband. After the extravaganza of planning our two weddings, one Hindu ceremony with 450 guests and one Catholic ceremony with 330 guests, I found myself unemployed and certain I could plan weddings for others and make a business out of it. So at the age of 23, I created Simply Weddings. Adulting was still fairly new to me, and our rent was annoyingly due every month. Simply Weddings was simply not making any money, and I was then inspired to be a nail technician. I rounded up the cash to take the training and three months later Nail Mobility was born. Get your nails done in the comfort of your own home, nail mobility will come to you. This worked out somewhat, and then I found a job posting for a nail tech in a foot clinic and spa. After three months of giving manicures and pedicuring some of the most unsightly feet for $10 an hour, the owner liked my work ethic and offered me the position of manager moving my salary up to $2500 monthly. Since we had just purchased a new home this was fantastic.

Shortly after, I became pregnant with my first child and my husband lost his job. Since I was on contract once the baby came, we had no income. Before meeting my husband, I had patched things up with my folks and we had moved close to them. Seeing our struggles, they lent us money to buy a photo finishing lab. Not realizing that digital was on its way in, the lab never made much money leading me to have to supplement our income. Now with two children this led me to become a children's yoga instructor and I started Earth Kids Yoga followed by A Royal Tea Party, an at home tea party business for little girls' birthdays.

As my life evolved and moved forward, I always came up with another business that suited my availability, my lifestyle and my passion. When developing my ventures, I was creating from something personal to me. Whether it was solving a problem I had experienced, or creating an affordable alternative to something I wanted to experience, or birthing a version of a service that treated the customers and clients the way I wished I was treated, or developing a program that was offered with love, integrity and care, it was always coming from something I myself had experienced.

I went on to create my Intuitive Healing Practice, then added coaching, an online radio show, an internet tv network, a life celebrations business, an online magazine, a line of healing products, a Law of Attraction pop album and to compose and record meditation music.

Being an entrepreneur allows you to create freedom for yourself and for those who benefit from your products and services. Being an entrepreneur gave me the key to be free to be me.

Charlotte Howard Collins

Award Winning Business Growth Expert | Speaker | Best Selling Author
Publisher | Entrepreneur
www.LinkedIn.com/in/charlottehoward
www.Instagram.com/coachwithcharlotte
www.Facebook.com/coachwithcharlotte
www.iamcharlottehoward.com
www.heartcenteredwomenpublishing.com

Charlotte Howard Collins is an Award Winning Business Growth Expert, Speaker, Best Selling Author, Publisher and Entrepreneur who helps WOMEN build successful and profitable businesses doing what they love. Known as the Business Breakthrough Strategist, she teaches things that are beyond college education.

Her journey from working as a full-time licensed hairstylist employee to becoming a successful female entrepreneur has inspired more than 5000 women globally to build their own businesses through her Heart Centered Women Publishing, Wealthy Women Enterprises, Wealthy Women Inner Circle, Hair Artist Association and Wealthy Women Entrepreneurs Network. She has received numerous awards during her entrepreneurial career, including the Top Transformational Women Leader Award, Best Entrepreneur Award and ICONIC Writer Influencer Award. She is a loving wife and mom to four beautiful children.

In her spare time, she loves going to the beach, reading, writing, listening to music, watching movies, traveling to exotic locations and cooking.

Self-Made Female Entrepreneur

by Charlotte Howard Collins

Want to know what sets the unstoppable women entrepreneurs apart from the wannabe women entrepreneurs?

It's not money, or brilliant ideas, or even powerful friends.

All those things (and more) are nice to have, but they're not a requirement of success. What is a must-have, though, is a good attitude. Without the proper mindset, you'll constantly be battling your own brain, and that's exhausting.

- You'll allow yourself to believe your ideas are worthless.
- You'll remain convinced that you aren't smart enough.
- You'll be certain that someone else did it (whatever "it" is) better.

Before you know it, you'll have talked yourself right out of launching your new program or book. In no time at all, you'll be back at your day job, working away on someone else's business because you don't have the confidence to create your own. I fell into the same trap several times before I decided enough was enough. I thought life dealt me a bad hand, but a simple mindset change can make all the difference.

Start Building Your Lucrative Business Empire, Not Another Job!

Many women dream of working for themselves and having the freedom to only take on clients and projects they love.

What they don't realize though, is that there is a huge difference between becoming an entrepreneur and being a self-employed business owner.

Women Entrepreneurs scale their income. Self-employed business owners trade hours for dollars.

Women Entrepreneurs leverage the skills and talents of others. Self-employed business owners rely only on their own skills most of the time.

Discouraged yet? Don't be. Most women entrepreneurs started out as a self-employed business owner while working on a 9 to 5 job. Just don't stay there. These tips will help you build a lucrative business empire instead of just another job.

1. Don't Try to Do It All Yourself.

Building an empire requires that you leverage the talents and time of others. While it might seem cost-effective to simply do everything yourself, especially in the start-up phase when you likely have more time than money, it's a path to burnout and stress.

Instead, separate your tasks into those that you love and are especially suited. Then make a solid plan to get those that you aren't good at off your list of things to do. If you can't afford to outsource it all right now, start with what you tend to procrastinate the most on, even if it's just a few hours each month.

2. Don't Allow Yourself to Work All the Time.

The trouble with working at home is that you live at work. That means that there's no clear line in the sand between your workday and your personal home life.

Since there's always work to do, it's easy to find yourself working every available moment, often to the benefit of your family.

You can help avoid this by:

- Setting and maintaining clear work hours.
- Having an office with a door you can close when you're done.
- Scheduling time for family and other activities.
- Taking time for yourself.

3. Vacations and Downtime Are Important.

Don't create an empire that requires you to be "in the office" every day. At the start, you may need to be available more, but you should be planning for when you can be "off the grid" for extended periods of time.

- Have a trusted team who can handle things when you're not available.

- Leverage automation tools and repeatable systems so you're not always re-inventing the wheel.

While you might not be able to hit the road with no internet access for weeks at a time, at the very least you should be able to reduce your workload to a daily check-in.

Sounds impossible? It's not. With some planning, you can create a team and the systems they need to successfully run your empire without becoming overwhelmed and overworked.

The last thing you want to do now that you've decided to finally leave the 9 to 5 job is to add more stress to your life. Isn't that why you decided to build your own empire in the first place? You're looking for freedom from your awful boss, nasty coworkers, and the limitations of a fixed salary.

If you're trading all that in for a different kind of stress, what have you really gained? Before you kiss your cubicle goodbye, be sure to build a solid foundation first.

4. Build a Financial Safety Net.

Nothing stresses us out quite like worrying about money. Whether you're concerned about how you're going to pay the mortgage or any other bill, it's easy to lose your mojo. As a new woman entrepreneur, you certainly don't want money trouble casting a shadow over your dreams.

Before you turn in your resignation, set aside some cash for a rainy day. Aim for at least three months of living expenses but more is better. Relieve the pressure of having a new business that's not earning.

5. Make Sure Your Family is on Board.

Money troubles are bad, but there may be one thing that's worse: an unsupportive spouse. Not everyone understands the drive to build an empire. Most women find it scary to step away from that regular paycheck to chase after a dream.

If that sounds like your husband, don't take it personally. They're not making a statement about your ability. More than likely, they're just worried about what the future holds. Do your best to understand where they're coming from, and be sure to explain your ideas, why you are confident it will work, and how you plan to cover the startup expenses and manage the risk.

6. Take Time for YOU.

No matter what's going on you need to be sure to schedule some "YOU" time. No one can work all the time, regardless of how driven you are. No one can stay healthy while maintaining a nonstop schedule. Take time away from your desk to rest and rejuvenate. Without it, you'll find yourself overwhelmed and stressed. If you want to build a successful and profitable business doing what you love, join my Wealthy Women Inner Circle Facebook Community at www.wealthywomeninnercircle.club

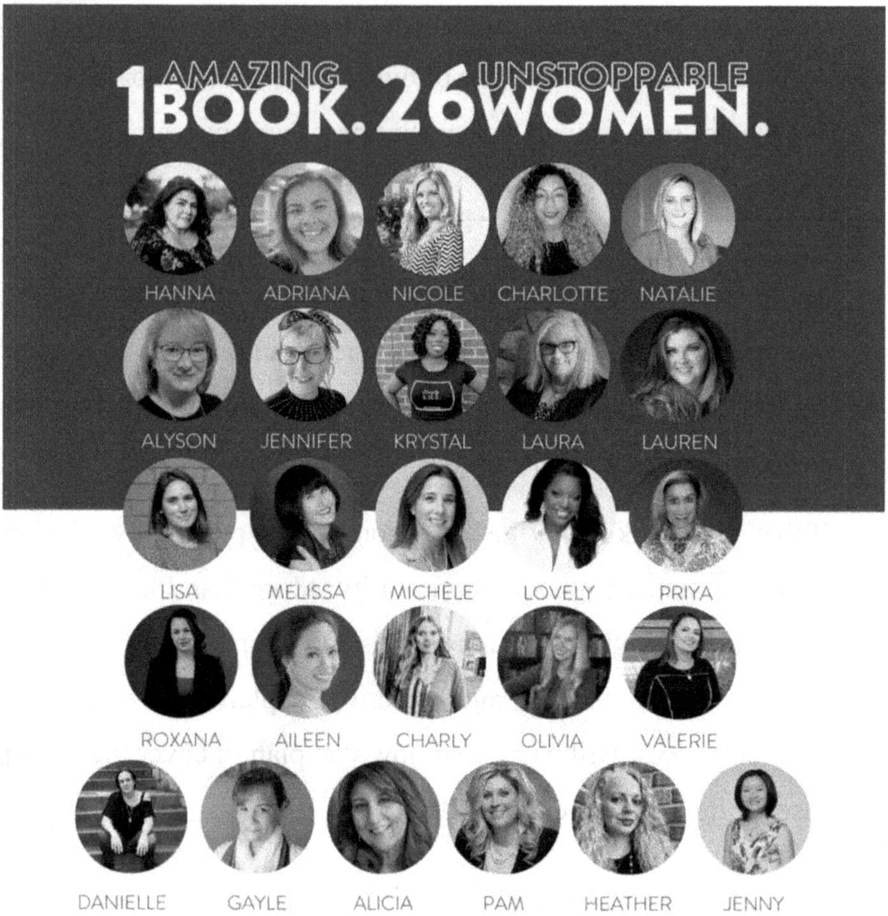

1 AMAZING BOOK. 26 UNSTOPPABLE WOMEN.

HANNA · ADRIANA · NICOLE · CHARLOTTE · NATALIE
ALYSON · JENNIFER · KRYSTAL · LAURA · LAUREN
LISA · MELISSA · MICHÈLE · LOVELY · PRIYA
ROXANA · AILEEN · CHARLY · OLIVIA · VALERIE
DANIELLE · GAYLE · ALICIA · PAM · HEATHER · JENNY

MADE BY ENTREPRENEURS FOR ENTREPRENEURS

There's a new wave of powerhouse women dominating the business industry, and we want YOU to learn about them. Each chapter was authentically written and represents each author's unique and innovative perspective on becoming an unstoppable woman entrepreneur, as well as the challenges we face as female business owners. Inside, you will learn applicable strategies, mindsets, and best business practices. Whether you're just looking to start a business or to expand and take things to the next level, this book is for you!

She Rises, She Leads, She Lives
Join the #BAUW Becoming An
Unstoppable Woman Movement
www.SheRisesStudios.com

JOIN THE MOVEMENT!

#BAUW

Becoming An Unstoppable Woman
With She Rises Studios

She Rises Studios was founded by Hanna Olivas and Adriana Luna Carlos, the mother-daughter duo, in mid-2020 as they saw a need to help empower women around the world. They are the podcast hosts of the *She Rises Studios Podcast, the* TV show hosts of *Becoming An Unstoppable Woman,* as well as Amazon best-selling authors and motivational speakers who travel the world. Hanna and Adriana are the movement creators of #BAUW - Becoming An Unstoppable Woman: The movement has been created to universally impact women of all ages, at whatever stage of life, to overcome insecurities, adversities, and develop an unstoppable mindset. She Rises Studios educates, celebrates, and empowers women globally.

Looking to Join Us in our Next Anthology?

Becoming An Unstoppable Woman Mompreneur

Visit www.SheRisesStudios.com to see how YOU can join the #BAUW movement and help your community to achieve the UNSTOPPABLE mindset.

Have you checked out the *She Rises Studios Podcast?*

Find us on all MAJOR platforms: Spotify, IHeart Radio, Apple Podcasts, Google Podcasts, etc.

Looking to become a sponsor or build a partnership?

Email us at info@sherisesstudios.com

www.ingramcontent.com/pod-product-compliance
Lightning Source LLC
Chambersburg PA
CBHW050635160426
43194CB00010B/1686